"There is nothing I would not do for those who are really my friends"

Jane Austen

The Friendship Book

A THOUGHT FOR EACH DAY | 2023

January

HE was a big, heavy man. His camouflage jacket was buttoned tightly around him. The hat, decorated with skulls, was pulled low on his forehead. The bandana across his face left just enough space to see the glitter of his eyes.

He might just have been wrapped up against the cold, but everything about his dress and demeanour said, "Stay away! Don't talk to me."

There were six concrete steps between the car park and the pavement. As I walked down, he stepped up purposefully, and was breathing heavily by step three.

"You'll get there," I said, speaking as if I had every right to.

"Oh, I'm getting too old for this," he replied.

"I know that feeling," I said with a little laugh.

At the bottom I looked over my shoulder. He stopped at the top and turned. He raised his hand in a sort of salute, and said "Happy New Year, mate."

For a second we were more than the camouflage we habitually wear; we were fellow travellers on the same difficult journey.

I could have taken his appearance at its word and said nothing, but how we look is so rarely who we are.

PRAGUE-BORN poet Rainer Maria Rilke stood on the roof of his lodgings in Capri at midnight to welcome the year 1907.

The next morning, he wrote to his wife, saying, "Let us believe in a long year that is given to us, new, untouched, full of things that have never been."

The possibilities, now as then, are endless and exciting. What good thing that we have never done before shall we do in this gift of a year?

Tuesday — January 3

IT'S time once more to turn the page
To see what lies ahead;
We make our peace with yesteryear
And put the past to bed.

Nothing's quite as sure as change;
We'll take things as they flow,
Trusting in a greater plan
That isn't ours to know.

The future is a mystery,
Its story yet untold,
But the present is a gift to share,
Worth more than any gold.

Laura Tapper

Wednesday — January 4

WE had decided to go for a longer than expected walk on a very icy, cold day.

"It is one of those things," Harry began, "that would probably have seemed like a terrible idea when I was warm and cosy at home."

"And yet," I offered, "we feel better for doing it."

"Aye, well." He blew on his hands. "We'll certainly feel like we've achieved something when we get home."

There are so many times in our lives when it seems like a better, easier idea to stay in a comfortable place, but there is no growth in staying comfortable.

There is no sense of achievement, none of the confidence that comes from not having taken the easy way.

Step outside and go a little further when you can.

You'll feel better doing it and you will feel great for having done it.

And the views along the way will more than make up for the effort!

Step outside and take a journey – you'll feel better for it!

Thursday — January 5

IN an era when very few people have "lums" and "reeking" is positively discouraged, what does the old Scots phrase, "Lang may yer lum reek" have to offer us?

In times gone by it was a New Year's toast, or simply a way of wishing someone the best – or, more accurately, wishing them all they needed.

If you lived in a croft in some isolated location, you might have been cut off by the snow or the sea and your pantry might be almost empty, but if you had peat, wood or coal for the fire, then everyone could huddle around it and wait the winter out.

A fire in the hearth and soup in the pot would keep the family going through tough times.

Smoke rising from your chimney told the world where you were and that you were still there. Perhaps it also said, "Come and join us!"

Our chimneys might not smoke as much these days, but "lang may yer lum reek" ought to remind us of just how little we need to get by, and to appreciate everything else we have.

Friday — January 6

THE little candle-in-a-tin smelled of oranges and pine trees.

The Lady Of The House and I had agreed, back in December, that it was the most Christmas-smelling thing we had ever caught scent of.

But I couldn't figure out why she slipped it into the bag we were packing the decorations away in.

"When it comes time to put them up again, I shall probably be very busy and not in the mood," she explained.

"I imagine that opening the tin and lighting the candle will be all the festive boost I need," she continued. "Besides, I heard someone say, 'Do something today that your future self will thank you for.' This is it."

Excellent advice! It already has me looking forward to December, but there are plenty of days between now and then to fill with gifts for our future selves.

What shall we do today – for tomorrow?

IN the youth of the year, I was thinking about the passing of wisdom from one generation to the next – and if it actually works!

A young friend admitted to some frustrations when it came to teaching his teenage son . . . well, anything!

He also remembered being the same sort of frustration to his own father.

"He was trying to teach me things that he had learned the hard way," my friend explained. "I told him that I wanted to learn from my own mistakes, not his. Well, my boy just said the same thing to me!"

Perhaps that's the way it has to be. Perhaps it's the only way that works.

Perhaps the best thing we can do as parents is not get angry and indignant when the next generation refuses our hard-earned wisdom.

Instead, we might keep the peace and stand by to help as they learn to stand up by falling down.

And while we wait, if we have learned anything, we might mentally apologise to our own parents.

ADMIRAL HYMAN RICKOVER was a United States naval officer of long experience.

He was a fan of a prayer that Breton fishermen would say before setting out in the morning.

He liked it so much, he presented the first two lines of it on a plaque to each submarine commander commissioned on his watch.

He also presented one to President John F. Kennedy, who kept it visible on top of the Resolute Desk in the Oval Office.

For each of them, it was a reminder of their place in the grand scheme and on whom they ought to depend.

The words on those plaques read:

"Oh, God, thy sea is so great and my boat is so small."

As we sail our little "vessels" through the vast sea of life, it's an idea worth remembering.

Monday — January 9

IN times gone past, this was Plough Monday. It often marked the return to work after the festivities of Christmas.

Perhaps to put that return off for just a little while more, in some areas the plough was decorated and paraded through the town.

Boys would dress as women, men would dress as clowns or fools, there would be dancing and singing, and a collection would be taken.

Thereafter, it was down to the hard grind of the agricultural life. Did they need their celebrations more in those days? They certainly deserved them!

And how nice that even the humble, hard-worked plough had its own day of glory!

Tuesday — January 10

HUGH has been expanding his woodcraft skills through the winter. On a notion he decided to become a spoon whittler. He's learned that the handles are difficult, but he has to be most careful with the "bowl" of the spoon.

Recently he learned that some specialist spoons come with holes or slots in them. Not being a cook, he'd never heard of such a thing.

"I thought the purpose of a spoon was to lift things in its bowl," he told me. "But now I find that a spoon that can't even do that still has uses in the world. I'll look at spoons – and people – differently from now on."

Wednesday — January 11

THE supermarket was obviously trying to get their customers used to less-than-perfect fruit and veg. The oranges, on a paper tray and shrink-wrapped with clear plastic, were odd sizes and had some superficial blemishes.

The label stuck on top described them as "Not the best, but still good!"

I hadn't been looking to buy oranges that day, but I put them in my basket anyway. Why? Because I knew how they felt.

Tools – and people – of all shapes and sizes have a role to play.

Shutterstock.

13

Thursday — January 12

THE little patch of woodland seemed absolutely bare, yet the sparrow still hopped from branch to branch in anticipation.

I emptied a small bag of seeds on to the leaves on the ground, then walked away to give him a little peace.

As I walked, not looking back, I spoke the words of the great poet Emily Dickinson:

*"Hope is the thing with feathers
That perches in the soul,
And sings the tune without the words,
And never stops at all."*

Friday — January 13

IN the first half of every January, Theresa and Kevin meet for coffee.

They bring their diaries. Friends from school days, they share highlights of the past year, then they "revive" the years and friends they had in common.

"It's maintenance," Theresa told me. "We believe that memories are the most precious possessions we will ever have, so we like to keep them in a good state of repair."

Saturday — January 14

I DIDN'T think ducks and frogs were your style." I pointed at the brolly tucked amongst more grown-up umbrellas in her hall stand.

"I don't remember who that belongs to," Catherine replied. "People always leave things here. Brollies, scarves, bags . . . My hubby thinks it's because they feel so at home that they think their stuff also belongs here."

I thought for a moment.

"You don't happen to have my cap, do you?

Catherine raked through a drawer and presented me with my "missing" cap.

We all want our houses to feel like home, but if they feel like home for other people, we know we've done something right!

Sunday — January 15

IT'S a message of comfort, attributed to the 16th-century friar St John of the Cross.

"I was sad one day and went for a walk; I sat in a field. A rabbit noticed my condition and came near. It often does not take more than that to help at times – to just be close to creatures who are so full of knowing, so full of love, that they don't chat, they just gaze with their marvellous understanding."

We might not know why someone is sad. But we do know how it feels to be sad, and in simply sharing the moment with them we show them they aren't alone.

Monday — January 16

I HEARD someone say, "The price of love is loss".

We seem to have accepted that as a sad truth, and it is a part of the package. But do we gain nothing for having loved and having been loved?

Is it just that the loss is so deep, so sharp, that it grabs almost all of our attention, leaving so little to appreciate what love caused to grow?

My sympathy is always with those suffering a loss, but my heart tells me love will always be a gain in the end.

Tuesday — January 17

JENNIFER'S first job was as a pool lifeguard at a holiday camp. It only lasted the summer, but it was fun and led to better things.

To do the job, she had to pass the Royal Life Saving Society's Bronze Medallion test, which was exhausting and quite an achievement.

We were remembering holidays and warmer days when she told me she'd recently rediscovered her medallion. She dug it out and I asked what the Latin motto around the edge meant.

"I only recently looked it up," Jennifer admitted. "It translates as 'Whomsoever you see in distress, recognise in him a fellow man.'

"Or woman," she added. "Words to live by, don't you think?"

I should say so!

OUR dear friend Mary is a voracious reader.

She is also, occasionally, what some folks call a wind-up merchant.

"I can never remember whether a life story written by the person themselves is a biography or an autobiography," she told me.

"I really ought to find out. In fact, I'm going to add it to the list of things I ought to do," she continued.

"That list is so long it's practically a book in its own right. I should get it published. I could call it my ought-to-biography!"

Thursday — January 19

YOU wake in the morning and shuffle into the kitchen. You switch the kettle on, then lean on the worktop by the sink.

You look out of the window and wonder if those really are snowflakes fluttering down. A robin redbreast lands on a fence post and sings, apparently just for you.

You just know it is going to be a good day, so you thank God for the world.

Then you thank your neighbour for keeping their bird-feeder well stocked.

Friday — January 20

HE was looking at his six-month-old mono-blocked driveway. The recent frosts had caused one of the many interlocking bricks to crack.

"Will you need to take that one out and replace it?" I asked.

"I was wondering about that," he replied, rubbing his chin. "But I think the bricks surrounding it will keep it in place and allow it to keep on doing a useful job. Don't you?"

I ventured that they almost certainly would, and walked on thinking what a perfect analogy for community that was.

Let's get beside and around all of our friends and our neighbours to hold us all together.

Saturday — January 21

*A*s long as the sun keeps shining
And sets in a golden glow;
As long as stars keep twinkling
And rivers continue to flow;
As long as there are raindrops
Refreshing all the land,
And the sound of soothing waves
Keep swishing on to sand;
As long as flowers keep blooming
And birds twitter and sing,
We will all have rainbows –
The best that life can bring.

Pamela Ramage

Sunday — January 22

THE world will celebrate Robert Burns and his inspirational words in three days' time.

Before he found fame, he told his father of the words that meant the most to him. They were in the Book of Revelation, chapter seven, verses 15, 16 and 17.

They talk about God living among us, an end to hunger and thirst, being fed and led by "the Lamb", and the Lord wiping all our tears away.

It's nice to know where the great poet-to-be found his inspiration!

Monday — January 23

IT should be today, in Utqiagvik in Alaska, that the sun will rise for the first time since it set 66 days ago. Being inside the Arctic Circle means putting up with a long mid-winter's night.

I imagine it takes some getting used to. I know people struggle with our long nights at this time of the year.

Utqiagvik, though, is an encouraging reminder that, whether our dark times are caused by the tilt of the earth or by personal circumstances, the sun always rises again!

Tuesday — January 24

HE was an unpleasant man. He brought out the worst in me. I asked him to tell me about his childhood and he ridiculed the idea that there was anything to be learned that way. Then he agreed to tell me one story of no importance or significance.

While emphasising its irrelevance, he told me the one thing that explained everything about him. My heart still breaks when I think of the loss he so flippantly described.

It reminded me of the words Henry Wadsworth Longfellow wrote in "Hyperion: A Romance":

"Every heart has its secret sorrows, which the world knows not, and oftentimes we call a man cold, when he is only sad."

Wednesday — January 25

A FOLK tale has river water evaporating from the sea and falling as rain on its source.

"I told you to go straight to the sea, but you went the long way," the source says.

"You did," the rain replies. "But you didn't have to face the rocks, the fissures, the swamps, the animals who would drink you, the humans who would divert . . ."

The point is, I think, that those who stay at home should be more understanding of those who go on the journey.

Thursday — January 26

HARRY was pruning his gooseberry bush when I felt the wind on my cheek and turned my palms up to catch some of the gently falling rain.

"Not really the best day for that sort of thing," I suggested.

"I have a coat and a hat," he said, shrugging. "Besides, the one who prepares for spring will feel its arrival long before those who are still hiding from winter."

I nodded and took myself indoors for a hot cuppa. It certainly didn't look like spring out there, but I remembered his words and wondered just what Harry might be feeling.

AT bedtime, all the lights turned off.
I stood there in the dark;
The frosted garden looked unreal,
With trees so bare and stark.
A frozen tableau caught in time,
The moonlight stripped it bare –
Just everything iced-crystal still,
There's not a breath of air.
And then the first few snowflakes fell
Like feathers from the sky,
Just floating, twirling, spiralling –
Like magic from on high.
I felt deep down that childlike thrill
That first snowflakes can bring;
Emotions filling up my heart
And making my soul sing.

Eileen Hay

Saturday — January 28

READ some uncredited words of wisdom on the internet. "Some stranger somewhere still remembers you were kind to them when no-one else was."

It reminded me of a man I met in a church café. He insisted we'd met before, even though I had no recollection of it. He told me he was doing well, working, much happier. It was good to hear, but I was still wary.

"That was a powerful talk we had back then. Those words made the difference," he told me.

"Remind me," I prompted, still unsure of him.

"You said, 'Just because you're down doesn't mean you're out'. I remembered those words and built on them over the years. You gave me hope."

Not such profound words that they actually stayed with me, but they would have been honestly meant, and whatever kindness I put into them at the time meant they could go on to do their work after I had left.

Sunday — January 29

THE Fitzwilliam Museum in Cambridge has a display of notation knives. The cutlery, from the 16th century, has music engraved on the sides of the blades. It's thought their purpose was to encourage thanks to God as the family gathered to eat.

A decent meal – many of us take it for granted. For many others it isn't guaranteed. If we didn't have our many blessings for a time, then they reappeared, we would certainly celebrate.

While we have them with us, whatever they might be, we could do a lot worse than sing.

Monday — January 30

HUGH was telling me about someone he talks to on social media. "He is helpful and supportive," Hugh said, "but I have no idea how he sounds in real life."

"How do you think you sound?" I asked.

"On bad days, I sound like someone who's been ill, waking up and saying hello to someone who's been caring for them and has just said 'Hey, there'. On good days, I sound like the person saying 'Hey there'."

I liked that. Good or bad, he heard himself as either end of a loving, caring situation.

We convey so much through our tone, it's worth remembering that our speech is about so much more than just the words we use.

Tuesday — January 31

POPPY is a lovely middle-sized dog.

"She's normally at the back end of the lead when we walk," her owner, Judith, told me. "She's that busy sniffing around. But give her a stick and she runs straight to the front, prancing, head held high. She carries those dirty old sticks like they are antlers, as if she is suddenly powerful, and she becomes the defender of our little herd."

It's an entertaining image, but it also sounds like Poppy understands the proper use of any sort of power: to defend.

A dog's instinct is to defend – what's yours?

Shutterstock.

February

I'M pretty sure I was walking through a cloud – and discovering my coat wasn't waterproof. My ears felt the chill from my sodden cap.

The "view" was of a building site. The few workers out seemed busy laying pipes to drain the rainwater into the nearby river.

The digger driver leaned out of his cab to talk to someone I couldn't see. Then I realised the other man was in a trench so deep that only his yellow hard-hat was showing.

God love you, sir, I thought, glad not to be in his wellies. And my day got better from that moment on.

It's a strange thing. Even while we complain, we know we are comparatively well-off, but sometimes we need to see it to believe it.

LOOK around and tell me what you see."

A busy road, litter, shops, a car park . . . I knew there was a river off to one side but couldn't see it. All in all, a fairly depressing view.

Harry, though, seemed to be paying special attention to the electrical substation. This was surrounded by a seven-feet-tall wall and a barred gate.

Beneath the sign warning of danger was a name. It declared that this bleak place was *The Woodwynd Granary*.

"Once upon a time," Harry explained, "this was wooded land. There was a track 'wynding' through it towards the grain store and the water-powered mill.

"Our world isn't always the one thing, although it can sometimes seem like it. If this place is having a tough time right now, it's good to remember it had better times in the past and it will have more in the future."

Take the long view, Harry was saying. The good times are never all that far away.

Friday — February 3

HAVE you ever felt "the ahhh-ness" of it all?

Then you might have experienced what the Japanese call "mono no aware", which means to take a delight in the beauty of all things while being sadly aware of their impermanence.

Most beautiful moments owe some of their beauty and wonder to the fact that they are fleeting.

Thankfully, there are always more to be found. The "ahhh-ness" keeps on coming. We just have to be aware.

Saturday — February 4

WHY are you here so early,
Shining all alone?
The other flowers sleeping,
Their faces yet unknown.
But you have bloomed this morning,
Your petals fresh and new,
Too young for this cold weather,
Now covered in winter dew.
Go back to sleep, my pretty,
And wait till spring is here.
When you can feel the golden sun,
Then you can reappear.

Lily Christie

Sunday — February 5

WHO am I kidding when I judge others?

If ever I was to find myself standing in front of an all-knowing God, I would probably be too busy shrivelling up with embarrassment to point the finger at anyone else.

Even if I didn't believe in such a god, there is someone else who knows every lie I have told, every selfish decision I have made.

Me!

Unless I forget or, as is more likely, choose not to remember.

So I ask again, who am I kidding when I judge others? God? Myself? It's surely one or the other.

Monday — February 6

SIMON had an unexpected day out with just him and five of his grandchildren.

"You wouldn't have got much work done," I suggested.

"I had so much work to do it gave me a headache," he said. "But I also had the chance to take the children out. I decided they were more important and went for it.

"When I got back home, the headache had gone. I got twice the work done in half the time."

Our paid work is important, but the work we do for love yields better dividends.

Tuesday — February 7

LOOKING out of our living-room window, I turned to the Lady Of The House.

"I don't know what's got into our cat," I said. "She's sitting out in the rain, staring at the fence. She was doing the same yesterday. I don't know if there are insects there, or if something else is grabbing her attention."

Then I realised.

She wasn't staring at the fence – she was staring through the trellis that tops our fence, straight at the three birds on our neighbour's bird feeder!

I'd been sure she was doing a silly thing, but she wasn't.

The next time I think I have someone figured out for better or worse, I am going to take an extra moment or two to make sure I understand how the world seems from their point of view.

Wednesday — February 8

I DON'T know if it was a genuine mistake, or if the sign in the station waiting-room had been altered by some wag.

I imagine it was supposed to say, *Please do not leave your belongings unattended*.

But what it actually read was, *Please do not leave your longing unattended*.

We should take time to see things from another point of view.

Shutterstock.

Thursday — February 9

T'S a notion of service rather than expectation. It's often credited to the great Scottish novelist Robert Louis Stevenson.

"Don't judge each day by the harvest you reap, but by the seeds that you plant."

Of course, the up-side of focusing on planting seeds is that, inevitably, you or those you love will also have a harvest to reap.

Friday — February 10

HE question, posted on social media, was, "What's the best compliment you had in your life?" Someone calling themselves Redelkrunning replied, "I have never had a compliment."

Within seconds, Boyroger42 replied to that, saying, "I like your name. It's cool."

To which Redelkrunning posted, "The best compliment I ever had in my life was from Boyroger42, who said my name was cool and it really helped with my depression."

So often it's the littlest things that make the difference.

Saturday — February 11

WAS a little under the weather and the Lady Of The House shared an extract from Great-aunt Louisa's diary.

Louisa suffered her fair share of the maladies of her time, without the medical advantages we have.

"We tend to think of ourselves as either well or ill," she wrote. "But on certain days we can do certain things. On other days we cannot."

Sometimes, we feel nothing will be achieved. At other times, the world is ours to claim.

The tide is not always in, nor always out. Mostly it is somewhere in between and all we can do is wait for it to change.

Listening to her read, I thought I felt the tide turn.

But I still put aside my to-do list and spent the afternoon on the couch, under a blanket, with a good book. Just waiting.

Sunday — February 12

HEARD that, in the early 1900s, an American department store employed a group of men whose sole purpose was to be fired whenever a customer complained about something.

I wonder how much it cost them not to improve their standards of service.

In the Book of Matthew, Jesus says, "I desire mercy, not sacrifice."

The easy way out of any situation is to throw money at it or blame someone else, but the better way is to raise our standards.

Practising mercy raises all that is best in us.

Monday — February 13

IT'S the sort of hearsay that I always hope will be true – because it speaks to how good we might be.

In the early days of the coronavirus scare, apparently China sent supplies to Italy.

On the boxes, they wrote a line from an Italian poem, "We are all waves from the same sea".

Around the same time Japan sent supplies to China.

On their boxes, they quoted a line of Chinese poetry, "We have different mountains and rivers, but we share the same sun, moon, and sky".

Tuesday — February 14

YOU don't have to buy me diamonds to show how much you care,
Or smother me with flowers, or flatter me with flair.
You don't have to make a gesture that's grand for all to see,
A gentle touch and "I love you" will do just fine for me.
You don't have to send me chocolates or buy a flashy car,
Or make candlelit dinners, or sing beneath the stars.
You don't have to show the whole wide world
That you're in love with me –
You show it every single day
And that's how it should be.

Linda Brown

We've survived since we were babies – we can keep going now!

Wednesday — February 15

IT'S just a tin lid, about two feet in diameter and decorated with a picture of leaves, plums and apples.

It was probably the top of some food container or other.

When Danielle found it, she was living in a sparsely furnished flat. It was lying in a pile of rubbish by the roadside.

She took it home, cleaned it, then hung it on her wall as a work of art. If you didn't know its history, you'd never be able to guess that it had such humble beginnings!

It's the way with so many things in this world. It's not what you look at – it's what you see when you look!

Thursday — February 16

I'M sure we've all seen videos of laboratory mice running through mazes.

A teacher in our local school made just such a maze for the class guinea pig from cardboard.

The children watched, excited to see what happened when "George" explored the maze.

He entered through the doorway, climbed up a wall, then skipped from wall to wall, following his nose directly to the waiting treat.

"What did the children learn?" I asked my teacher friend.

"That they don't always have to take the path the world lays out for them. If, like George, they have talents that allow for a better, shorter, or quicker way, then they shouldn't be afraid to use them!"

Friday — February 17

MY friend Liz watched her new nephew, Oran, kicking his feet in the air, then turned it into a lesson for others.

"If you feel you've just been surviving life, just treading water, remember this day. You kept yourself afloat and alive. Well done! When you finally get to dry land, when your circumstances change and your feet hit opportunity – you will be off!

"All that treading water will have built up your strength. And there will be no stopping you!"

Saturday — February 18

HOW often were we told as children that it's rude to stare? Perhaps we shouldn't stare at people, but is staring itself necessarily such a bad thing?

After World War I, Walter J.C. Murray became disillusioned with London, and sought a home for himself in the middle of nowhere.

Copsford House was a ruin described by the farmer who owned it as "a mile from anywhere".

Murray spent a year there, immersing himself in the natural world. He earned some income by finding, drying and selling herbs. Later he would write a book, "Copsford", about his experiences.

But I was talking about staring.

It was at Copsford that Murray learned to do more than look.

"I slowly learned to stand and stare," he wrote. "I not only stood and not only stared, but I began to see. I saw lovely things and rare things . . .

"I caught an occasional glimpse of the intricate and complex pattern of life, and once or twice, as fleeting as the rainbow-flash from a trembling dewdrop, I perceived that all these things were but the external signs of a kingdom such as I had never dreamed of; that these colours were as a drop-curtain which, while it might never rise to disclose the stage within, grew transparent before my wondering eyes." ("Copsford" by Walter J.C. Murray, 1948.)

Sunday — February 19

ADVICE can be deep and spiritual, but if it's not practical, is it any use?

Sergei Sakharov was a Russian Orthodox priest who established a monastery in Essex, England.

He died in 1993, and left behind many words of wisdom, but he captured the popular imagination with this advice, given to another, possibly grieving, monk.

"Stand at the brink of the abyss of despair, and when you see you cannot bear it any more, draw back a little and have a cup of tea."

Now that is advice that surely all of us can take on board.

The good old cup of tea is a much under-rated remedy for all sorts of difficult situations.

Monday — February 20

SOME graffiti can be ugly, some can be beautiful, and some just makes you feel good!

Walking through the city on a dismal day, I saw, painted on a gable end, the words, *Thank you for the sunshine you add to the world.*

I smiled and wiped the rain off my face.

Thank you, my friend, whoever you are, I thought.

Tuesday — February 21

ANCIENT as I am, I can remember the days of bin men swinging metal dust bins on to their shoulders and emptying them into dust carts.

I remember people complaining about the noise! As if those bins only contained dust and could be handled delicately and silently.

These days, most of us have plastic wheelie bins and leave them by the kerb-side, but I doubt that a refuse collector's job is much easier.

I smiled when I brought Jane's bin back in for her and saw she had painted a big flowery "Thank you!" on the lid.

She never sees the people who take her refuse away, but that's not going to stop her showing her appreciation. There's always a way!

Wednesday — February 22

IN the middle of the film "Singin' In The Rain", Gene Kelly's character turns to the producer and says something like, "And there's one more scene."

There then follows one of the most epic dance routines in movie history.

I turned to the Lady Of The House and said, "You know . . . that had nothing at all to do with the plot of the film. It was just another excuse to dance."

My sweetheart looked at me quizzically.

"Is there a problem with that?"

No, actually, there isn't. In fact, if we are able, we should grab every opportunity to dance that we can! That sort of joy is above and beyond "plot".

Thursday — February 23

A WALK in the woods in February is an interesting experience. Lacking the cover of their foliage, we see the trees are different shapes and sizes, grow into the spaces left by others and reach for the sunlight in whatever direction it comes through the canopy. Some fall or are broken, then start growing anew.

We accept them all as valid, even important, parts of "the wood".

May we be as charitable with those of our own kind who, because of their own constraints and circumstances, fail to grow as society expects them to grow.

Friday — February 24

THERE is so much emphasis placed on achievement in life! Achievements are important, but shouldn't overshadow everything else. This is why I like this idea from Kurt Vonnegut's 1963 novel "Cat's Cradle".

"Life is a garden," he wrote, "not a road. We enter and exit through the same gate. Wandering, where we go matters less than what we notice."

Perhaps the real purpose of our achievements and our wanderings is simply to provide new things to notice . . . and wonder about.

Saturday — February 25

WHAT does friendship mean to you?
Does it lift and warm your heart?
Does it comfort you by night?
Does it help the day to start?
Just a kindly word or deed,
Now and then a cheerful smile,
An unexpected card or letter
To make life's journey so worthwhile.
Never underestimate
The friendship you have found,
And share the love, the hope and joy,
Then spread it all around!

Iris Hesselden

What does friendship mean to you?

Shutterstock.

Sunday — February 26

WHAT'S the shortest verse in the Bible? People generally answer "Jesus wept", John 11:35.

At nine letters long, it's the shortest verse if you read it in an English translation. But it's 16 letters long in Koine Greek, the original language of the New Testament.

In the same language, 1 Thessalonians 5:16, "Rejoice always", has only 14 letters.

Being the shortest verse has no significance, but the fact that the answer can be looked at from two points of view, and be so very different, reminds me that the same approach can be taken to life.

Do we look at the things of this world and weep, or do we rejoice? It depends on how we choose to "read" this thing called life.

Monday — February 27

THERE'S a saying generally credited to Persian mystic Rumi: "What strikes the oyster shell does not damage the pearl."

I suppose what he meant was that we can't control what the world will do, what people will say, and what accidents occur, but they might impact our "shell", leaving dents and scratches.

But we are not the shell – we are the beauty inside the shell. The superficial is just that, and we should stay beautiful where it matters.

Tuesday — February 28

AN artist showed me around his studio. His paintings were impressive, but my attention was grabbed by a frame around a switch on the wall labelled *Self-belief*.

When I asked about it, he laughed and said, "It's not connected. It's just a little home-made thing – but then so is self-belief.

"You're taught it by people who will believe in you at one time and not at another. But the person whose belief you need the most is you! When I feel overcome by doubts, instead of going into a fug, I click the switch and remember – I believe in me!"

I bought a painting, but the switch wasn't for sale. Perhaps I'll make a version of my own. I believe I can!

March

WRITING to John Newton, the minister and hymn writer, the poet William Cowper recalled a public flogging.

A man was sentenced to be dragged through the town behind a cart, being whipped all the way. The beadle, a soft-hearted chap, applied the punishment lightly. With each stroke, he ran the whip through his hand, which was coated in ochre to give the appearance of an angry welt.

Seeing this, the constable who had arrested the man started hitting the beadle with his truncheon. In response to that, a young woman started slapping the constable. And so they proceeded, all through the town.

It's a good illustration of two things. The first is that the ripples of one unjust deed will usually be more than we could have imagined.

The other is that, in the world at large, there will be people who fight for justice and people who fight for mercy. Therein lies the cause of much conflict – and our only hope!

STORIES from the 1936 Olympics tend to focus on American runner Jesse Owens, who defied Hitler's notions of racial superiority.

But I also like the story of the Japanese pole vaulters, at the same games, who tied for second place in their event. Because Shuhei Nishida and Sueo Ōe were friends, they declined the chance to compete against each other. The judges awarded Nishida (who had cleared the height in fewer attempts) the silver medal and Ōe the bronze.

Pleased, but not content, they took their medals home, and had a jeweller cut them in half and join them so they were half silver and half bronze. They called them the "friendship medals".

An Olympic medal would be worth having, but a friendship medal surely beats all the rest.

THIS woman stands before me,
So confident and sure,
And I have loved her all her life,
With love so deep and pure.
Her childhood flashes through my mind,
My pulse begins to race,
My heart melts at the joy I see
Reflected in her face.
As she takes those cautious steps,
Proud tears I try to hide,
As I watch my lovely daughter,
Today become a bride.

Elizabeth McGinty

Saturday — March 4

YOU might have heard the notion that if we smile when we don't feel like it, it actually encourages the chemicals that cause us to feel better.

I have tried it before, and whether it's from laughing with embarrassment at myself or something else entirely, it does seem to work.

This is why I was intrigued to hear of an old Taoist practice of developing an "inner smile".

From what I understand, it's a way of always being a friend to ourselves.

It means having a part of ourselves set aside from the physical world.

This part of ourselves is there to tell us things like "well done", "never mind" and "you're still loved", no matter what is happening at that moment.

I might not have the proper understanding of it, but I like what I do understand.

A dependable, reassuring, encouraging smile, for yourself, from yourself.

To me, that sounds like something well worth developing – so why not give it a try?

Sunday — March 5

ELENA needed help. She didn't go as far as counselling, but she did talk to a sympathetic colleague.

She explained the pressures she was under, and how, occasionally, they would spiral out of control, meaning that her work and her relationships suffered.

"But," she explained, "when I have my life together, I'm a good person."

The colleague looked puzzled.

"Don't you realise," she asked, "that even when you don't have everything together, you're still the same Elena? You are still a good person."

Simple words, but they looked beyond the nonsense – and they played a huge role in helping Elena make things better.

If a perceptive person could see to the heart of a woman like that, how much more will God understand the heart of each of us, whether we have our lives together or not?

Monday — March 6

A SHORT ferry crossing on a windy day reminded me of advice given to me when I was a lad and took a few tentative steps into the world of sailing.

"Sailors get their 'sea-legs' by learning how to walk with the rise and fall of the deck."

This life is no fixed and stable path. It will have its ups and its downs. But we will travel further and better by not planting our feet too firmly.

Tuesday — March 7

SOME artistic soul painted words on a board and hung them from a branch in the woods.

They read, "Everyone wants to be the sunshine to brighten up someone else's day. But, don't forget, you can also be a shining moon in someone's darkest hour."

Shine brightly or shine gently. Each will be needed in its own time.

Wednesday — March 8

SHE'S a special helper at a busy airport. People with physical, emotional and psychological needs go to her for assistance.

We chatted for a while, I watched her help several people, and I think I fell in love with her a little.

She was so ideally suited to the job of being someone to care in difficult situations.

Then she mentioned she had retired from her previous employment because of an invisible disability.

This job actually helped with that condition; it kept her mind engaged, it kept her body working and, in her words, "it keeps my heart warm".

Helping others – it is always the best way to help ourselves.

Thursday — March 9

GIOVANNI GUARESCHI, the author of the Don Camillo books, wrote in Italian, then his books were translated for the appreciative English market.

But in "The House That Nino Built" (1953), he uses a Latin verse, and either he or his translator writes it as "Tomorrow is another day."

I'm sure we'll all be familiar with the phrase, implying that things will be better later, but the Latin he used was *Incipit vita nova*, which means "Here begins a new life".

Why wait for tomorrow to make a difference? The best time for a fresh start is always now.

Friday — March 10

HE had travelled widely, this friend of mine, and mostly on foot. He had visited many towns and had a secret way of figuring out how long he would stay in each.

"If the stray cats or stray dogs were friendly and relaxed, I knew it was a place with a majority of good, kind people and I could happily stay a while.

"If not, then I passed through as quickly as I could."

THE farmer and his wife had converted a barn to a tea room. I sat by a window with a cuppa, gazing outwards.

It wasn't really the time of year for scenery, and rising hills cut the view short. There were some fields, hedges and a row of bare trees separating land from sky. Nothing much.

I had been lost in it for the best part of 20 minutes, and felt all the better for it.

Returning home afterwards, I took John Ruskin's "The Moral Of Landscape" from its shelf.

I found where the English art critic and designer had written these words:

"How delicious to the feeling heart to behold so fair a scene of unsophisticated nature, and to listen to her voice alone, breathing the accents of innocence and joy!"

When it comes to letting nature (and a cuppa) refresh your soul, it really doesn't take much.

FEW people use the lonely path; it goes by quiet ways,
But on that day it suited me, my mind lost in a daze.
I sat awhile upon a rock, my problems hounding me,
And tried to see the way ahead, wherever it might be.
Then idly lifting up a stone, I saw a curious sight:
A tiny coin was nestled there, some ancient widow's mite.
I rubbed it with my fingers to clean its faded lines,
And recognised the letters: it had come from Roman times.

I wondered at the person who last held it in their hand,
But accidentally lost it here, amidst the mud and sand.
I marvelled as the clouds around my heart began to lift;
It even made me smile to see this unexpected gift.
I had a sudden thought, and took a coin of my own,
And put the two together there, beneath that self-same stone.
Perhaps someone will find them, two thousand years from now,
And the joy of it will wipe troubled furrows from their brow.

Ewan Smith

Monday — March 13

THE traffic lights at the crossing were out of action. Drivers were taking their best guesses as to whether to stop or go.

Then an elderly man, leaning on his walking stick, approached and stood there looking puzzled. Of course, there was no light for him, either!

A young man stopped his car, got out, waved to other drivers to stop, then helped the other man across the road. Everyone else waited. No-one tooted.

Bless him. Bless them all. A simple kindness, of no great note in the grand scheme, but wonderful just the same.

If we gave the green light to more acts like that – if we encouraged them and promoted them – we might change the world by them!

Tuesday — March 14

ACCORDING to popular legend, a customer at a Tim Hortons in Canada paid for his order and the order of the customer behind him in the queue. That customer did the same. And so began a three-hour-long chain of kindness, involving 226 people.

Now, the quicker thinking and perhaps more cynical of us will point out that only one person, the one who ended the chain, actually benefited financially. But how many people had their day made? And how uplifted were the staff?

Wednesday — March 15

ABBOTSFORD, where Sir Walter Scott lived, is now a popular visitor attraction and well worth a visit.

One of their displays is a box of rusty keys gathered from the house during renovations. Presumably, each of them once guarded things someone thought precious or wanted kept secret. Now, they serve no purpose except as a display showing the age of the building, because that treasure and those secrets are long gone.

Thus time casually disposes of the things we would keep locked away.

As far as is practicable, we live a better, more open and honest life if it is unlocked.

Historical sites are full of unexpected treasures.

Abbotsford House, located in the Scottish Borders, was once home to the writer Sir Walter Scott.

Shutterstock

THE Lady Of The House was having one of our smaller angels fitted for shoes.

I waited outside on a bench, and my attention – never focused at the best of times – was taken by a seagull. Perhaps it thought it spotted a snack.

I watched as it swooped down from the sky, grazed a paving slab with a feather-tip as it turned, then rose and disappeared.

"I have always wanted to do that!" the man beside me said.

"What?" I asked.

"Fly," he explained, with longing in his tone. "I have always wished I could fly!"

As we exchanged a few more words, I looked at him and saw nothing much on the outside worthy of comment. But on the inside he dreamed of flight!

We never know. We think we can tell. But we really can't.

DAFFODILS on my doorstep
Greeted me today,
Bright as morning sunshine,
Although the skies were grey.

Two bunches tied with ribbon,
I picked them up with care.
I hadn't heard the doorbell . . .
Who could have left them there?

But once I found the little card
It all became quite clear.
The writing was unmistakeable –
"Spring flowers for you, my dear!"

Ah, friends make all the difference.
I felt my spirits sing
At this lovely gift of kindness,
Holding promises of spring!

Marian Cleworth

Saturday — March 18

A **GROUP** of friends meet up for breakfast at the local café every other Saturday. They are good men with a variety of interests, so the chat is usually lively.

They live ordinary lives, which is nothing to be disparaged, but none of them have achieved anything of great note. Yet they know with certainty what the Prime Minister, the President, the Chancellor and the managers of various top-level football teams ought to have done.

I thought of my friends – and myself – when I saw this anonymous offering:

"The best way to succeed in this word is to act on the advice we would give to others."

Sunday — March 19

J **ESSIE** showed me a picture of her and her mother with her mother's mother.

Sitting by the older woman's feet was Jessie's daughter, Freya.

Scans confirmed that Freya was expecting a daughter. Five generations, although only four were visible.

So it always has been, and so it always will be. Motherhood is the immortality of the human race.

One day of appreciation a year isn't nearly enough, if you ask me. Because it's no easy task and isn't always smooth sailing.

Happy Mother's Day to mothers everywhere!

Monday — March 20

É **TIENNE DE VIGNOLLES** was a supporter of Joan of Arc. He was known as "La Hire". It may have been a nickname from the English soldiers he fought, who saw him as "the wrath of God", or "Ira Dei". It may also have come from the French word *hérisson*, which means "hedgehog", because he was a prickly character.

Why do I mention it? Because while a healthy self-respect is a good thing, a conceit of ourself can leave us open for a fall. One minute we are the wrath of God, the next we are a hedgehog!

Tuesday — March 21

I SAW a bin lorry of a type I'd never seen before, and I thought of an ill little lad – all of two years old – who, when he's well enough, likes to climb on his window ledge to watch refuse collectors go by.

I took my phone out and explained the situation. As I recorded, the refuse collectors set their machine into its unusual lifting and crunching motion.

Job done, these busy, cold and hard-working heroes lined up in front of the truck, called my young friend by name, and gave him a get-well-soon cheer!

Gentlemen, you brought a lump to my throat and brightened a child's day. Thank you!

Wednesday — March 22

DURING the Austro-Prussian War of 1866, the principality of Liechtenstein fielded an army of 80 men. Its part in the war was protecting a pass that no-one tried to cross. Then they came home, and the army was disbanded shortly afterward.

But the event entered into popular legend when the army returned home with no casualties and one more man than they left with.

It's supposed that the extra man was an "enemy" liaison who liked Liechtenstein so much that he wanted to live there.

The reality was probably more complicated, but the story reminds me of words generally credited to President Lincoln:

"Do I not destroy my enemy when I make him my friend?"

Thursday — March 23

ONE of my neighbours took in a parcel for me. It was a rainy day and the cardboard box got pretty wet in the process.

When I went to collect it later, I saw it sitting on her coffee table wrapped up in a tea towel.

I doubt she'd put much thought into it, but I did.

How we are with the little things in life so often accurately reflects how we will be with the big things.

It doesn't take much to brighten a child's day.

Friday — March 24

SOCIAL reformer Sophia Sturge, of whom was written, "Never, perhaps, were the active and passive virtues of the human character more harmoniously and beautifully blended than in this excellent woman", died in 1845.

Her brother's friend, the poet John Greenleaf Whittier, wrote these words of advice for him:

"With silence only as their benediction,
God's angels come
Where in the shadow of a great affliction
The soul sits dumb!"

Sometimes, doing nothing is enough. Silence is a gift, but you can't offer it from a distance – you have to present it in person.

Saturday — March 25

THERE'S a tale of a woman who meets a hungry traveller. He asks for food, so she opens her bag and tells him to help himself. There's bread in the bag, and also a jewel that could set him up for life. He asks for it and she gives it to him.

Months later, he returns the jewel and begs for something more valuable.

"Whatever it is within you that enabled you to give away such a treasure!"

What we can't give away, we are a slave to. Be free!

Sunday — March 26

IN his poem "Comfort", Robert W. Service described a man, down and out, with no-one to care for him and no-one to care for.

The poet spent years wandering the west coast of Canada and America writing of the highs and lows of gold prospectors. Often his own condition was no better than the men he described, but he ended the poem with a reminder we might all take comfort from.

"Yes, if you're a tramp in tatters,
While the blue sky bends above
You've got nearly all that matters –
You've got God, and God is love."

Monday — March 27

HE looked like he'd walked a hard road.

Several layers of ragged woollens separated him from the wind and the rain.

I asked him what his day had in store.

"This is my day for being out among the poor," he said. "I've got some helping to do."

His words made me consider the familiar story of the widow's mite.

"All these people gave their gifts out of their wealth," Jesus says, "but she out of her poverty put in all she had to live on."

Then I walked on, humbled and yet uplifted.

Tuesday — March 28

I WAS reminiscing with my good friend Harry about coal fires from our past.

As children we were often the ones sent for a fresh shovelful when the fire died down.

"I remember holding the handle with both hands," Harry explains, "trying so hard not to drop any.

"I can still hear the 'shhhh' of the lumps as they slid off the shovel. I would be content if only one or two pieces hit the guard and fell on to the fireplace. They could easily be picked up."

His face developed that faraway look.

"I often worried," he explained, "that the fresh shovelful might be too much for the fire.

"Think about it – those coals were exhausted. They had given almost their all, and here I was, dropping a great weight of rocks on them.

"I worried I might put them out," he continued. "But, of course, they recovered, and the fire burned brighter because of that extra weight."

Was he making a point about how the things we see as burdens are often blessings in disguise?

He would hate for me to suggest he was anything like that fanciful, but still . . .

Every life must be appreciated – even the lonely tree.

Wednesday — March 29

THE ornamental gardens were bare, the trees were silhouettes, th
paths were empty and a gentle rain had just begun.

I stepped into the shelter, hoping to wait the shower out. From
there I could see a plaque bearing some words of John Muir, the Scot
who helped establish the American National Park system.

They read, "In every walk with nature, one receives far more than
one seeks."

What had I received on this cold and seemingly empty day, I
wondered.

I leaned back, resting my head against the brickwork of the
sheltering wall. I was warm enough, hadn't over-exerted myself and
there was no place I needed to be any time soon. I breathed deeply.

Peace, I realised. Completely unasked for – I had received peace.

Thursday — March 30

WHEN the weather's dreich, Gill's children put on their
waterproofs and walk up a nearby hill to visit the Lonely Tree.

It's the only tree for a mile around and is exposed to the worst of
the weather.

"The children understand that life everywhere deserves to be
appreciated and encouraged," Gill told me. "So they try to make
sure the Lonely Tree isn't!"

An example worth following. And not just for trees!

Friday — March 31

HUSH-A-BYE, baby, on the tree top" is one of the best-known
nursery rhymes in the world. It's thought to date to a Native
American practice of hanging babies' cradles from branches to let
the wind rock them.

This reminded me that in "When A Man's Single" by J.M. Barrie,
the main character sits a baby cradle across a stream with a paddl
attached so the water would rock it.

It's nice to think we have been taking advantage of renewable
energy – wind and waves – for a long time.

April

GREAT-AUNT LOUISA'S diaries present her father as a gruff man. Recalling a double wedding, she said the date was picked to suit his other commitments.

It was Louisa's sister who was to be married, but Father decided her brother should share the event – despite him not yet having proposed to his sweetheart!

The celebration didn't break the bank, but there was nothing anyone could call Father stingy for, and he ran the event with a happy precision. Then Great-aunt Louisa wrote:

"Those of us remaining having done a useful degree of tidying, Mother handed out candles for our holders. Father took the ring of keys from the hook, preparing to lock the front door.

"Instead, he sat on a bench. I heard the keys slowly being turned around the iron ring for the next hour. I think he could hardly bring himself to secure the house with two of his flock still on the outside."

Fathers. They might pretend not to be emotional creatures, but ꓳuisa knew better.

MS In The Desert" is a wonderful book of devotionals, ꓳed by Lettie Cowman from the writings of her husband, Charles Cowman.

have dates from the 1940s. While the intended writings oiration, I also take heart from the unintended writings.

pages have scribbles in coloured pencil, and inside in the shaky script of someone learning their ⁄ords "Bambi" (the Disney animation had just been ꓳlom" (meaning peace).

ꓳ wisdom ought not to be reserved for the ur children might understand them better!

Monday — April 3

HAVE you ever seen an old lace-maker's bobbin? Made of bone, they might be five inches long.

They were often weighted at one end with "spangles", i.e. beads or small stones on a wire loop.

Every once in a while you find one whose spangles were more than just weight and decoration.

Some weavers attached spangles that meant something to them, like a button from a wedding dress, a child's tooth, a gem from a mother's earring or a shell brought home by a travelling husband.

Bobbins were used for weaving, but they often carried the warp and weft of life with them as well.

The 19th-century equivalent of home-made charm bracelets.

Tuesday — April 4

HE had a clip-board in one hand and a golf umbrella in the other. The wind pushed and pulled at him as he searched for his car keys.

"It's a day for keeping a tight grip," I suggested.

"Aren't they all?" he replied grimly.

And I was reminded that the same day can be a breeze for some and a storm for others. Be sunshine wherever you can.

Wednesday — April 5

*W**ITHIN** my tiny garden there's a table and a chair –*
It's where I love to sit and dream, when there's time to spare.
I breathe in scents of earth and stone, of green and growing things,
I listen to the insects' hum; a blackbird as he sings.
A rambling rose surrounds my seat; I'm hid from every eye,
No outside world disturbs my calm, no cloud obscures my sky.
And here I come when fuss and fret seem set to overwhelm,
For this is where my heart's restored, within my garden realm.

Maggie Ingall

Thursday — April 6

RYAN showed me a picture of his two-year-old son, holding his toy JCB digger – actually sitting in a JCB digger!

"How did you manage that?" I asked.

"They were resurfacing our road," he explained. "The digger driver saw the toy and the look of awe in my son's eye. He invited him on board while I took some pics to prove it happened."

The driver explained his kindness, saying, "I loved diggers when I was a boy, and I would have loved someone to do this for me."

Needless to say, the little lad was beside himself with excitement.

Oh, if only more of us would remember what mattered to us when we were children! The world might be a happier place.

Friday — April 7

THE borders and public gardens where she lives are full of bushes chosen for their hardiness and prickliness.

Their (minimal) care involves chainsaws and leaf-blowers. Children don't play in them and they offer little for the bees.

But every time I go to visit I see new plants peeking through or interesting specimens coming into blossom. I know who planted them there. And – officially – she probably shouldn't. I'm not going to tell.

Tired of the thorns, her solution was not to rail against them, but to plant flowers.

Saturday — April 8

ONE bright morning, I overheard two old countrymen talking. One had just handed in his fortnight's notice at work.

The other was bemused.

"What you bin and done that for?" he asked. "A man don't want to leave a place where he could allus say he liked hisself."

No doubt the first man had his reasons for moving on, but I liked his friend's philosophy.

Let us always strive, whatever our situation, to live life in a way that allows us to like ourselves.

Sunday — April 9

THE massive wooden cross hung by near-invisible wires from the cathedral roof. An artist friend commented how the white linen draped over it contrasted well with the hard lines of the cross.

She said it should always be "dressed" like that.

I told her it was only done that way at Easter-time to depict the cloth left in the empty tomb when Christ rose.

But I liked her point. The cross does symbolise the harsh brutality of the world, while the linen is like his grace: light to bear, softening everything, flowing everywhere.

Monday — April 10

A BELL-RINGER told me of an old tradition in some counties of announcing a death by pealing the church bell once every five minutes for an hour.

"The bell started 'mouth up' and finished the same," he said. "Gravity, grease and a little pull on my part took care of the ending. But raising the bell to that position in the first place was heavy work. I had brawny friends I could call on for that part.

"'Talking' of a death like that took time, thought and teamwork. I wish when people talked about other things they took the same care."

Tuesday — April 11

I COMPLIMENTED little Elsie on her plaits and her bows. She twirled around, making them fly. Then she wanted to tell me all about the brush and the mirror.

"They were silver! And they had roses! And they brushed the tugs out like magic!"

"They were my gran's vanity set," Elsie's mum told me. "I remember them being on her dressing table, and I remember the first time she brushed my hair with them. I felt so grown up – and so loved!

"They're not real silver and the roses are painted, but they belonged to my gran. Now they belong to Elsie's gran. I think that's where the real magic lies."

Wednesday — April 12

MY phone accidentally took a screenshot of a conversation I had with one of our neighbours.

I noticed it long after I had forgotten what the conversation was about.

She had seemed to think my spirits needed lifting.

I could see where she said, "Reap what we sow, so you will undoubtedly have many friends willing to help.

"And it's raining. Bring your washing in."

I had to laugh before deleting it.

Friends who can be encouraging, philosophical and practical in the space of a few short sentences have to be among the very best.

Thursday — April 13

IN the days when most houses in the countryside were thatched, it was believed that with "a good hat and a good pair of shoes" a house might last hundreds of years.

By that they meant a well-tended thatch and firm foundations.

It strikes me that, especially on the colder, wetter days, a good hat (or an equivalent way to prevent the weather getting in) and a good pair of shoes will keep most of us going until the sun shines again.

Friday — April 14

IN Rudyard Kipling's classic novel "The Jungle Book", Baloo the Bear teaches Mowgli the man-cub the "Master Words of the Jungle".

Mowgli learns to say them in the languages of the elephants, the bears, the hawks and the snakes, so that, saying them, he would be safe among those creatures.

What were those "Master Words"?

They were a statement that would make the whole world safer and happier if humans took it seriously.

They were, "We be of one blood, ye and I."

Saturday — April 15

HE was pushing the supermarket trolley with one hand and holding his daughter's hand with the other.

He kept close to the wall as they walked, to let other shoppers pass by.

The girl, who looked about two years old, was skipping and hopping and twirling.

"It must take a while to get anywhere with such little legs," I suggested.

"It does," he replied with the hint of a sigh. "But when she gets where she's going, she has always had plenty of fun along the way."

Great thinkers will tell you what that "tiny dancer" already knew. The journey is as important as the destination, so we may as well dance.

Sunday — April 16

HAVE you ever simply sat beneath a tree?

I don't mean picnicking, or reading a book, or talking to friend. I mean simply sat.

Now that the weather is picking up slightly, I might try it again, myself.

The wonderful Indian poet and philosopher Rabindranath Tagore had this to say about just such an experience.

"With patience, you revealed creative power in its peaceful form.
Thus we come to your shade to learn the art of peace.
To hear the word of silence."

A universalist, Tagore believed that certain basic truths could be found throughout the religions.

How much, in spirit, does his description sound like the Bible's "Be still, and know that I am God"?

We could, each of us, do worse than find a tree to sit under and contemplate the wonder and mystery of its creation.

I would say we might move on from there to contemplating the wonder and mystery of creation itself.

I have a feeling, though, that to fully understand and appreciate a tree might just take longer than most of us have to spare.

Each new day is like a new jigsaw puzzle.

Monday — April 17

WHEN Hugh moved into his new house, a large part of the garden was taken up by an old tree. It was covered in ivy, blocked the sun and branches fell in the wind. He decided to cut it down.

Then a visiting friend commented how nice it was to see an elm tree again after so many had been lost to Dutch elm disease.

What had just been a tree to Hugh before now had a name. He looked up its history, learned how it fitted into the local ecosystem, then he started researching how to care for it.

A name makes a difference.

Whether it's a situation we are dealing with, or a person, don't deal with them as strangers – learn their name.

Tuesday — April 18

GEORGE BERNARD SHAW wrote that "Youth is a wonderful thing. What a crime to waste it on children!"

Thinking of Great-auntie Mary causes me to take issue with the worthy playwright. Living well into her nineties, Mary never really lost that mischievous twinkle that caused us to love her so when we were children.

I happened to be present when she died, and heard her greet her long-since-passed mother in the voice of a child, glad to be home.

Youth! That blessed state will have us at whatever age we choose to have it!

Wednesday — April 19

WE had been buying our newspapers and bread rolls. Leaving the shop, my dear friend wore a thoughtful expression.

She looked towards the rising sun and took a deep breath.

"You know, the day is like a jigsaw. We waste a lot of time and happiness trying to create the new day from the broken or left-over parts of the previous one. If we walk forward in trust, the new day will provide enough pieces to paint its own, brand-new scene."

I took her advice and we walked into the new day.

Thursday — April 20

A *VERY* fine sampler still graces our hall;
We don't know the story behind it at all,
Except it consists of fine stitches so neat,
The sewer's clear talent presenting a feat.
My mother says once it hung near to her bed,
She'd memorised words learned by rote in her head,
"The Lord is my shepherd," there quoted in lines,
Familiar verses I've read many times.
But the pictures around it are what draw us in:
Sweet sheep with kind faces, the years cannot dim,
A sampler that has weathered long tests of time–
I'm glad it's still with us and now it is mine.

Judy Jarvie

Friday — April 21

H *E* took a slip on the tiles of the swimming pool changing-room. Both feet went from under him.

He landed on his posterior with a thump.

Giving him a hand up, I commented on how quiet he'd been.

"I might have shouted out, or said something I oughtn't to."

"Me, too. Normally," he replied with a grimace. "But my grandson is sitting in the changing cubicle and he thinks more highly of me than that."

Isn't it nice to have someone whose expectations we actually want to live up to? Is there anything better for us in this world?

Saturday — April 22

I **DON'T** know what playground mischief had been committed, but I heard the teacher's response.

"That's no excuse. I was seven once and wouldn't have done that. Never mind. You'll soon be eight."

His point was, I believe, that when we know better, we do better.

Now there is a wonderful philosophy that might apply to us all equally between the ages of seven to eight – and ages seventy to eighty!

Sunday — April 23

I'M sure we all know the verse from the letter to the Philippians that reads, "Finally, brothers,whatever is true, whatever is noble, whatever is right, whatever is pure, whatever is lovely, whatever is admirable – if anything is excellent or praiseworthy, think about such things."

It's highly likely that the Benedictine monk and founder of Clairvaux Abbey, Bernard of Clairvaux, was familiar with them, and had them in mind when he wrote the following practical advice.

"If you notice something evil in yourself, correct it; if something good, take care of it; if something beautiful, cherish it; if something sound, preserve it; if something unhealthy, heal it."

It would be easy to read those words then go on about our day, but if we took them seriously and gave them the consideration they deserved we might find something there that applied to us.

If we acted on their advice, what a difference that might make.

Monday — April 24

STACEY was cleaning for an older man. His wife had passed away a year before.

"Long enough," he said, "for me to get a little frayed around the edges."

That's when she noticed the hem of a trouser leg hanging down. Worried he might trip, she asked if his wife had owned a sewing box.

She had. It was still there.

The hem had been repaired before, probably by his wife. Stacey could have pulled the thread out and repaired it properly.

But, instead, she took the older, broken thread, tied it to the new length, and continued the work.

"It wasn't about gender norms," she told me. "Not about sewing being a woman's job.

"It was more about showing solidarity for a sister who would have done it if she could – but death prevented her."

Two threads tied together. Two women across the generations.

And one man, probably oblivious to the fact that they both, in different ways, thought he was worth caring for.

Tuesday — April 25

A FRIEND and I were having a deep conversation about how the church had lost its way and was more interested in ticking boxes than establishing real relationships.

A man I knew nothing about, except that he had problems, wandered over and made a couple of hesitant friendly comments.

I replied, and my friend said, "Anyway, Francis. As I was saying . . ."

I let him go on, then I held my hand out to the other man.

"I don't know your name, but it's nice to meet you."

He told me his name and shook my hand. My friend introduced himself and the three of us went on from there.

I hope my friend saw the "church" in what I did.

Wednesday — April 26

FOR maybe 10 days the bus stop in our street was out of action. I passed it today, when things were back to normal, and thought it could do with weeding!

The grass had reached over on to the tarmac, weeds had sprouted between the kerb stones and the base of the pole was overgrown.

I have never seen council gardeners working on bus stops, so I can only assume the passengers getting on and off the buses, day after day, do the job while being completely unaware of it.

Sometimes the good we do is like that. We do it unknowingly, simply by turning up!

Thursday — April 27

HE said, "I haven't seen you for a while."
I made some non-committal reply.

He kept talking, gradually working his way around to, "What was your name again?"

We had never met before.

What he was actually saying was, "Can I talk to you?" Then he told me about his wife leaving.

He just needed to talk. So I listened.

Friday — April 28

HE'D spent a lot converting an old barn into a home. It hadn't gone smoothly, but he was proud of what they'd achieved.

Parts of it still had the feel of a building site, but he felt he had found a for-ever home.

"Some folk might be less than impressed by it," he told me. "Well, we see what we want to see. But I believe our heaven is within us."

Those words stuck with me. Some folk could travel the world and never find heaven. Some will find it in a muddy field.

Contentment – it's ours to lose or to find.

Saturday — April 29

WE had a conversation on a sensitive subject. She talked carefully and listened. I talked and listened.

Where different strands of the conversation ended probably told each of us all we needed to know about the other's point of view.

"Of course, all that matters is love," she said along the way. "That's what I think. I know other people think differently."

If credit were mine to give, I gave her credit for those things.

After that chat, about something we disagreed on, we talked about other things, and we parted friends.

It can be done. We don't always need to fall out when we disagree.

This way, the door is wide open for future chats.

Sunday — April 30

THERE was an old tradition in the south of England where a shepherd would be buried with a tuft of wool in his hand.

The thinking was that this would show his occupation when he reached the pearly gates.

If he hadn't been to church as often as he might, the Lord would understand it was because he had been out caring for his flock.

It doesn't happen these days, but I imagine that most of us, standing at those gates, would like to tell the great shepherd of the lambs and wayward sheep we had spent our time caring for.

May

Monday — May 1

IT'S a centuries–old tradition, nowadays not often seen,
But they're setting up a maypole here on the village green.
The children from the school arrive, spring flowers in their hair,
And they skip around in circles, holding ribbons in the air.
The music and their dainty feet make such a lovely sound
As they weave strands into patterns: over, under, through and round.
The dance is done, the children smile and curtsey to the crowd.
The maypole's decked in colour. The applause is long and loud.

Vivien Brown

Tuesday — May 2

THE Lady Of The House and I were talking about conversations we could, or should, have with others but don't, because even though we can see the path to a happy outcome, the initial stages might involve resistance and upset.

It would be worth the effort in the end, but those first moments are awkward and difficult to walk into voluntarily.

This afternoon, I went upstairs to do some exercises designed to help with a temporary injury. I spent the first half hour lying on the bed, thinking about how much they might hurt.

I did them, and I'll keep doing them as I believe the end result will be worth it, but taking that first step was difficult – painful even.

If you are going to have those conversations, if you are going to improve your health, if you are going to make something better, have courage!

More than that, proceed gently, with love both for yourself and the others involved. Expect the process to be messy at first and try not to make it worse than it needs to be.

Keep your eyes on the goal, which should be a future situation even a little bit better than the present one.

Wednesday — May 3

THE palm tree was only a little one. It grew to about eight feet tall before a storm almost uprooted it.

For several years afterwards, various kind people propped it up with wood and ropes, but it still sat at a 45 degree angle.

I didn't see it for a further two years, but when I did . . .

From near the base of the trunk, a new branch had sprouted.

I say "branch", but it looks like it will be as thick as the trunk soon enough.

It is growing perfectly upright, and soon it might even be the tree!

Sometimes all we need is some support, just for a while, to get us through to that point where we can do better.

Thursday — May 4

THE food bank has a cat. Strictly speaking, it belongs to a couple who live in the neighbourhood, but it waits at the door every day.

It comes in, gets fed (like so many others) and curls up to sleep beneath the administrator's chair (unlike the others).

I wonder if it senses that this is a good place?

It's a lovely thought that, if you are doing the right thing, the world will find a way to let you know.

Friday — May 5

JACKIE is one of the Lady Of The House's oldest friends.

A few years back she presented my sweetheart with an embroidered cushion to symbolise their friendship.

Depicted on the cushion were two girls in love-heart-patterned dresses.

Now, there's a certain little cheeky charmer that we look after from time to time.

He's only eighteen months old, but he knows what he likes – and he loves that cushion. Now it is his regular cuddle-in-thing at naptime.

All of which is just to say – kindness spreads in unexpected ways!

Though a rare sight now, the maypole dance still brings joy in abundance.

Saturday — May 6

I ASKED Harry how his sciatica was.

"Oh, it's gone," he replied. "I hope it never comes back."

"It's just that I noticed you were still limping," I explained.

Not a man who likes to be caught out, Harry shrugged.

"I noticed that, too. I suppose I developed the limp to help ease the pain. Now the pain is gone, my body sometimes slips back into that habit, just in case."

I suggested that we develop all sorts of coping mechanisms to deal with all sorts of hurts. The trick is to leave them behind when we leave the hurts behind.

It isn't always easy.

"I'll work on it," he told me.

It's all we can do.

Sunday — May 7

THE retractable bridge had been opened, leaving a 30-foot gap between the two sides.

A gull sat on the roof of the far side. It spread its wings – no more – and the wind lifted it and it glided to the roof of the near-side section. There was a bridge in that gap. It was made of air, and only there sometimes.

I couldn't see it. I couldn't use it. But the gull was familiar with it.

I wondered how many more bridges are out there, how many more ways to cross seemingly impassable gaps?

God alone knows. And he will make them visible at the right time.

Monday — May 8

I USED to get told off for day-dreaming," Mary informed me. "But is there a better alternative? We have no control at all over what we dream in our sleep.

"At least when we are day-dreaming we get to choose what we dream about, and think about how to make them a reality.

"We must dream! So why not do it while we are awake?"

Tuesday — May 9

PEOPLE were gathered around, laughing, and photographing something in the supermarket car park.

I gave in to nosiness and saw two seagulls, in a beak-lock, assuming a tug-of-war position.

By the size of the crowd, they must have been there a while.

Each was in a braced position. Those big webbed feet would shuffle a couple of inches forward, then a couple of inches back.

There was no food involved. It's not like they were fighting over a chip or anything.

Each had a tight grip on its opponent's beak and showed no sign of being the first to give up.

Then a bigger seagull swooped down, squawked at them, and scared the fight right out of them.

Man isn't the only creature that will fight for no reason, but it was a good reminder of how foolish it looks.

And a reminder of how much we need a good "squawking-to" when we do it!

Wednesday — May 10

*I **WONDER** what to write about;*
I wonder what to say,
Except I think of you so much,
Remember you each day.
I think of all the times we shared,
The people we both knew,
How very quickly time went by,
So swift for me and you.
Remember long and sunny days
When all the world was young?
And how we laughed and shared a smile
As many songs were sung?
So treasure all these memories –
They're yours to hear and see,
And now and then just spare a thought,
A happy thought for me!

Iris Hesselden

67

Thursday — May 11

IT'S a small town, but we live at either ends of it.

It was raining quite heavily, so I phoned instead of walking over.

"Oh, it's not raining here," he informed me.

"Really?" I asked. "How can that be?"

"The rain has to stop somewhere, you know!" he said with a laugh.

That was many years ago, and I remember his comment still, when I find myself in one difficulty or another.

The rain has to stop somewhere. Perhaps, if I walk a mile in the direction of a friend, things might be brighter.

Friday — May 12

IN tales and legends, people seeking wisdom make epic journeys to find a guru living in a cave in some lonely mountain. Why?

It's supposed that they learn wisdom on the journey. But what about the gurus? Why do they live so far away from anywhere?

Perhaps they need to go that far to get away from the people who remember the mistakes they made on their own way to wisdom.

If someone lives and learns, we negate that by focusing on their mistakes. Focus, instead, on what they learned.

Saturday — May 13

TWO parents were watching a junior football match on a Saturday morning.

One turned to the other and asked, "Which one's your child?"

"Why?" the other one replied.

"So I can tell him how rubbish he is," the first parent replied.

"Why would you do that?" the other parent asked. "How would you like it if I did that to your child?"

"Well, you've been doing that all match," the first parent said.

"Who's your child?" the other parent demanded.

"The referee."

It always pays to think before we speak!

Days can feel brighter
with a friend by your side.

Shutterstock.

69

Sunday — May 14

IN her 1966 book "Sweet Vernal", Jean Margaret Peace wrote, "I am so content in country places that I lose the outlines and confines of myself and am diffused into the air. You see, there is always heaven close at hand."

Heaven is always closer at hand than we expect it, and the wonder of time spent in the countryside is that it reminds us we are more than the restrictions life sets around us.

We are part of a greater, God-created whole.

Monday — May 15

THE rain was washing the high street, but there were still plenty of people out in it.

I noticed one woman. She walked with a stick and her face told of her discomfort as she made her way along the pavement.

Our eyes met and I smiled. She smiled back. It seemed sincere.

Do you think it made a difference?

Further on, two women waited on opposite sides of the road. The green man appeared and one woman carefully lifted her walking frame on to the road.

The other woman met her three-quarters of the way across the road, saying, "Oh, Sarah, isn't this awful? Isn't it hellish?"

Do you think it made a difference?

If we don't think the difference is ours to make, then why do we speak? Why do we smile?

If we think it is, then might we be more conscious of it? Might we be kinder about it?

Tuesday — May 16

IT was a telephone helpline, and I happened to be standing behind one of the operators. She was wearing a head-set, so I didn't hear what the person she was talking to apologised for, but I heard her response.

"That's OK," she said sweetly. "We all have different skills."

That's kindness worth emulating and wisdom worth remembering.

I'M sharing this story even though I'm sure it must be fiction.
In the early 1900s, a minister was shepherding a parish in a far-flung part of Scotland.

On his way to church one morning, he stopped at the home of a "shut-in". He and the woman had a good chat on matters spiritual, then, before he left, he said, "Shall we have a word of prayer together?"

The woman agreed, but suggested he bring her neighbour in as well.

"Neither of us get out enough to do anything that would trouble the Lord, so one word of prayer will do for the both of us."

Nothing like getting your money's worth out of a prayer!

I have been surprised many times in my life by things completely unexpected, and when I have told friends about my amazement, they have replied, smiling, "Oh, we were praying for that for you."

A word of prayer, it seems, covers more than most of us could possibly expect.

IN his memoir "Country Boy", written about life in England before World War I, Richard Hillyer introduced us to his grandmother.

After a long life of poverty and loss, she "formed her own estimate of herself". Having had enough of drudgery, she decided she would be a lady.

She had no money, but she wore her Sunday hat and shawl every day, and took to strolling in the countryside, collecting flowers. When the weather turned inclement, she would sit elegantly in the church porch until the sun returned.

Such behaviour caused problems when other people didn't agree with her estimation of herself. But who knows better than us who we ought to be?

After a life lived almost exclusively for others, she had some time to appreciate herself.

It might be an interesting exercise to decide who we really want to be – and see how much of that we can make come true.

Friday — May 19

THERE'S an island in Loch Leven where, according to local legend, people who were at loggerheads were taken – and left!

Only when they had settled their differences could they signal the boatman to bring them back home.

The absence of distractions and the plentiful supply of time probably helped them reach their agreements.

Given how much we have in common as human beings, it shouldn't take such extremes to bring us together.

But it's nice to know the island is there – just in case!

Saturday — May 20

HE walked into the food bank and I assumed he must be from the local council, or some such. He was well-dressed and didn't look like he needed help.

I waited for him to speak to one of the organisers. When he took a seat by himself, I wandered over.

It turned out that he did, indeed, need help. The fine clothes he was wearing were the only clothes he had left. So we helped.

Judging "books" by their "covers" works both ways.

Sunday — May 21

I REMEMBER a story where an alien decided to bring peace to Earth. He began with two men who were at war over ownership of a fresh-water spring.

He asked them to stop. He explained how both would benefit. Eventually, he threatened them with destruction if they didn't stop.

So they stopped – until he left. Then they began fighting again.

It occurred to me that he could have used his awesome technology to dig each man a well.

Our faith might be thought of in the same way. We might proclaim it to be "the way", and we might broadcast it to the world, but if it doesn't demonstrate a noticeably better way to live, then we shouldn't be surprised when other people keep doing what they've always done.

It's not always plain to the eye who might be in need of help.

FOOD
BANK

73

Monday — May 22

FAITH is what the gardener knows,
With every little seed he sows:
Nurtured, watered, fed with care,
The roots and shoots will soon be there.

And so, it follows, in this life,
When times are dark and full of strife,
Somewhere will shine a ray of light
That leads us from the dark of night

Into a new day, fresh and whole,
And faith is what will feed our soul.

Elizabeth McGinty

Tuesday — May 23

YOU might know the statue in Piccadilly Circus in London as Eros, but it might actually be the Greek god Anteros.

The statue, sometimes known as the Angel of Christian Charity, is a memorial to Lord Shaftesbury, who presided over many charities, making life a bit gentler for those who had little or nothing.

A tale is told of a man who was to meet the lord at a railway station.

He asked how he would recognise the gentleman and was told, "Look for a tall man who is helping someone."

He did. Sure enough, he met Lord Shaftesbury for the first time.

The Angel of Christian Charity is a rather grand title to go by, but "someone who is helping someone" is something we could all aspire to.

Wednesday — May 24

SOME wit once said, "Salt is stuff that, if you don't put it on your potatoes, it makes them taste awful."

How many things that we take for granted go into making our day a good and pleasant one? Mightn't we spend a little thought on becoming aware of more of them?

Thursday — May 25

UNDER trees where buzzards nested, I found a starling wrapped in a fishing line. It panicked when I picked it up, but soon calmed.

I untangled it and put it on the grass. It sat for a moment, gathering its wits, then flew away.

I saw a red admiral butterfly in a puddle, trapped by the surface tension of the water on its outspread wings.

I put my hand in the puddle, palm up, and watched it crawl over my fingers.

Then I saw its wings ripple as they dried in my body heat. I put it on a buddleia bush, where it would find food aplenty.

I saw a daddy-long-legs on the floor, looking into a corner of our bathroom.

It tried to climb the tiles and fell. It tried to climb again and fell again. The third time it fell, my left hand was under it.

My right hand covered it while I walked out into the garden. I lifted the covering hand and it returned to the breeze.

We must seem like beings of infinite power to so many of the creatures we share this world with.

Be kind!

Friday — May 26

SUDDENLY through evening hush
Came the glorious song of a thrush.
Rippling chords through the cooling air,
His harmony hanging everywhere,
The aria he so often rehearsed,
A fountain of sound to quench my thirst,
Pellucid notes that soothed my soul,
Persuading me I was once more whole.
Smoothing away my jagged fears,
Drying my cheeks of salty tears,
Dismissing the discord and the strife,
Renewing my hope and joy of life,
Easing my mind from life's frantic rush,
Healing balm in the song of that thrush.

Ann West

Saturday — May 27

I HAVE forgotten the name of the plant, but I remember how excited Caroline was to show me it flowering.

"I've had it for a while," she said, "But it never really took. The slugs kept eating it before it could establish itself."

"What's different now?" I asked.

"I moved it," she replied. "The slugs don't go over there. Who knows why, but now it's had the chance to come into its own."

Wonderful! And a lesson for us, as well.

Sometimes, in order to thrive, we need to move away from the people and the situations who, for reasons of their own, like to take a bite out of us!

Sunday — May 28

W RITER, theologian, art critic and philosopher G.K. Chesterton wrote, "Faith means believing what is incredible, or it is no virtue at all."

"Incredible" is how the creator of the universe and everything in it would really need to be. Would anything less than unbelievable be worth believing in?

Monday — May 29

T HE rain was bouncing off the tarmac and the wind was whipping the branches of nearby trees.

I could have kept my head down and plodded on, but I looked to one side, where a gap in a hedge showed a vista of fields and open countryside.

Where the rain had been before arriving in our town, the slate-grey sky was a backdrop to a vivid double rainbow.

For a few uplifting moments, the entire curves of both bows were visible.

If I had started the day with the offer of a drenching in exchange for such a view, would I have taken it? Of course I would!

The "deal" we are offered by difficult times isn't so obvious. We need to look a little closer, but the rainbow will be there somewhere.

Tuesday — May 30

SHE was collecting wildflowers from the side of the lane.
Because her mother knew me well enough, the little lass felt she could confide in me.

The flowers were for Granny, who was at home in bed, not well enough to go walking with them.

She told me she had a nice vase picked out for the flowers, they would go on the bedside cabinet, and "Granny will smile at them."

Because she was so young, I did wonder if she had misspoken. Surely her gran would smile because of them, not at them.

Then I thought again.

At that age, to have Granny smile at you must be the greatest delight – the proof positive that you are special and loved.

I think she said what she meant and, in Granny's smile, she was offering her flowers the very best her little world had to give.

Wednesday — May 31

IT was a sparsely attended funeral. He had not been a well-liked man, often in trouble, keeping people at bay with his temper.

I imagine there were many who were glad to hear that he was gone.

The minister dealt with the spiritual aspect of it all; I only shared a story by the graveside.

I don't believe he ever told it to anyone else, and when he told me he insisted it meant nothing about anything.

It was of a great wrong done to his mother – something that had caused her to withdraw emotionally from the world, including him. He was eight years old.

In his never-again-fulfilled need for her love, he grew to resent and then to hate her.

From there it was only a short step to hating the world.

Was I making an excuse for him, you might wonder. It doesn't matter any more.

But I have in mind a reunion of mother and child in a place where love is undamaged and abundant.

I have in mind that he is home again.

June

Thursday — June 1

THE way children question everything, especially the things we completely take for granted, might be an annoyance to some parents, but it is a constant delight to me.

I was happy to be invited to the birthday party of a four-year-old friend recently.

When her mum asked if she wanted to blow out the candles on her cake, she asked, "Why would I do that?"

I think she rather liked the flickering lights.

"Well, you can't eat a cake with candles burning on it, can you?"

I remember being told that the candles number the years we have lived. We blow them out to signify that they are now in the past.

I'm not sure if that's the real reason, but I can't think of a better one, and hopefully the year ahead will be a piece of cake!

Friday — June 2

*I*T'S handy travelling in a car (that's if the roads are clear).
The weather's not a problem and the shops all seem so near,
But I have a suggestion that might come as quite a shock:
Instead of jumping in the car, be bold and try a walk!
You may well hear some birdsong and no doubt see some trees,
You might meet up with next door's cat, or come across some bees,
A spider's web upon a bush, some flowers just in bloom,
A workman whistling cheerfully some unfamiliar tune.
There's nothing like a walk; it's an adventure through and through.
Will you bump into some friends today or else meet someone new?
And think of the advantages: no need to pass a test,
No petrol fumes or traffic jams or feeling tired and stressed.
It doesn't matter where you're from, Blairgowrie or Bangkok,
Your life will be much better if you leave the car and walk!

Ewan Smith

Saturday — June 3

IF I was in a busy nightclub with a pint of beer, and someone bumped my elbow, I might spill some beer.

If I was at a delicate tea party and tripped over a cat, I might spill some tea.

Life has a (far too frequent) way of jostling us and making us stumble. What, then, spills out?

Well, it will be what we have filled ourselves up with!

Will it be anger and annoyance, or sunshine and happiness?

Sunday — June 4

I TALKED to a shepherd who, back in the day, had set out to medicate a flock of 200 sheep.

It turned out he only had enough for 180 of them, so he left them wandering the hillside overnight and returned the next morning to medicate the other 20.

"How could you know which had been dosed and which hadn't?" I asked.

He looked at me as if I were crazy.

"Because I know all my sheep," he replied.

Out of 200 identical (to most of us) sheep, he found his 20, because he knew them.

Isn't it a comfort that the Great Shepherd, with the whole world to care for, knows each of us individually?

Monday — June 5

WHEN we eat bread in our house, it often comes from a business that sells such items for less than the shop price, because the products aren't "pretty" enough to be on supermarket shelves.

But they taste just as good and they nourish just as well.

In the same way, people's behaviour might not fit social norms, or their looks might not fit with other people's expectations of beauty, but their hearts might be as loving as anyone's.

Look deeper, and prepare to have our spirits fed in the process.

Imperfections have never stopped Big Ben's bells from being evocative.

Tuesday — June 6

DIDN'T know either man, but I do know that at least one of them is a thinker.

We passed in a car park, and one man said to the other, "How's the day going?"

"Could be better. Could be worse," the second man replied a little wearily.

"What would make the difference?" the first man asked.

"Hmm," came the thoughtful reply. "Me, I suppose."

I suppose that applies to each of us every day.

Wednesday — June 7

FEELING a little imperfect? Not up to the job ahead?

Big Ben (the bell behind the clock) has been ringing the hours and the quarter hours for over a century and a half. It's an audible symbol of London the whole world over.

And it has been cracked for almost all of that time!

The sound it makes isn't the sound the foundry workers wanted it to make – but it's a fine sound nonetheless.

Thursday — June 8

I WAS walking with Caitlin, a four-year-old friend of the family, when she stopped and stared at a fence post.

I moved closer and looked over her shoulder at the tiny creature walking across the wood.

"I wonder if Aiden has seen a ladybird yet," she said softly.

Aiden is her baby brother. He hasn't been around long enough to have seen many things, but his big sister knew that he would be amazed by ladybirds – and surely by so many of the other things he has yet to see.

It occurred to me that I have been around for a much longer time than either of them – and I still haven't seen everything.

I don't think even the longest-lived of us does that, so it is probably always too soon to be shutting down our sense of wonder.

Friday — June 9

I DON'T know many people like him. I could wish I knew more. He has a soft heart, but is not easily taken in. He knows when to stay quiet and when to speak with conviction.

He has faith in a better world, but has walked in the darker corners of this one. He is always thoughtful.

He is best described in the words of the 17th-century poet Francis Quarles, who wrote: "Be wisely worldly, be not worldly wise".

The wisdom of this world, I am sure you will agree (and I am sure my friend agrees), is of a secondary quality.

Be aware of it, but be aware also that there is a better option.

Saturday — June 10

IT was an observation on a photo of a workmate's granddaughter. "Her eyes tell it all," he said. "She knows love. Like all people should, but . . ."

I knew what he meant about that look. I have seen it – and I have not seen it.

Childhood is really when it needs to be "installed". Once there, I don't believe it ever really fades away.

We can help give that, you and me.

Sunday — June 11

I PLACED eighteen-month-old Connor's hand on the Etch A Sketch and drew around it.

Then I suggested that he add some stars. He had covered some of his previous drawings by enthusiastically applying a star-shaped stamp.

This time he seemed a little more restrained. Thoughtfully, he added a single star to each fingertip.

I was reminded of the Graham Kendrick song "The Servant King", which contains the line, "Hands that flung stars into space".

I doubt that Connor has ever heard the song, but perhaps he knew something deeper.

Monday — June 12

THE wind inflated the shopping bag I'd placed by my feet.

I tried to stop it by stepping on it. It dodged me. I danced a few steps and tried again. The bag swerved away.

After it avoided my foot for the third time, I considered the possibility that the wind swirling around my legs was causing eddies that kept the bag one step ahead of me.

So I waited for the bag to settle, then picked it up.

I thought about the philosophy that we shouldn't chase our desires or we risk pushing them away, and how we ought to wait for them to come to us.

Chasing after the bag had definitely helped it to avoid me. But, somehow, I couldn't imagine that it would have come back to me by itself on such a windy day if I had simply waited for it.

So, as usual, the solution seems to lie somewhere in the middle.

Pursue your goals, but with thought and grace, and not with anything that might resemble me galumphing across a supermarket car park!

Tuesday — June 13

A FEW years before he died (in his mid-twenties), I talked to Andrew about his lifestyle, pointing out that it was no friend to him.

He said something that stayed with me.

"I know you think you have a better way to live. I'm sure you do. But I was born into this lifestyle.

"My parents were in it before me. My aunties. My uncles. That's what is real to me. Your way of life is . . . well, just a theory to me."

That shook me. It was a theory he never took a risk on.

How do we show people a better way? Whether it is a lifestyle, a faith or whatever.

To make a difference, we must do more than simply talk about it. Instead, we should invite them into it, include them in it and freely share it with them.

Even if only to show them that it really is worth taking a chance on.

Wednesday — June 14

EXPLAINING his interest in folk tales, writer and geologist Hugh Miller talked of a childhood passion for reading, and a shortage of books in his village.

Once he had read every book, he turned to his neighbours.

"Old grey-headed men, and especially old women, became my books; persons whose minds . . . had gradually filled, as they passed through life, with the knowledge of what was occurring around them, and with information derived from people . . . who had been born half an age earlier."

Miller lived in Cromarty in the 1800s, but I have a young friend, also an avid reader, who visits sheltered housing complexes in her own area, and asks the residents to tell tales of their lives.

Books are wonderful, but sometimes other people really contain the best stories.

Thursday — June 15

I HEAR there is a proverb in-east Africa that says, "Let your love be like the misty rains: coming softly but flooding the river."

It's a beautifully descriptive saying, but I spent a moment wondering about it.

Then I understood how a misty rain can flood a river – the same way love overcomes seemingly immovable obstacles. By looking like no threat at all, but not stopping, and never giving up!

Friday — June 16

HELEN KELLER lost her sight and hearing in infancy, but went on to become a world-renowned speaker, author and civil rights activist.

She is often quoted as saying, "I seldom think about my limitations, and they never make me sad. Perhaps there is just a touch of yearning at times, but it is vague, like a breeze among the flowers."

Can you imagine having such a sense of appreciation for good things that the loss of two senses would seem like an breeze among a life that is otherwise full of flowers?

I think I might try a little harder to be grateful today.

Celebrating music is a wonderful way of bringing us all together.

Shutterstock.

85

Saturday — June 17

WAS at a meeting and the host handed me a cup of tea in a corrugated cardboard cup. How very ordinary.

It reminded of the poet Ian McMillan, who called a cup of tea a lake he could float in, and described that first cuppa of the day as being where style meets substance; himself being the style and the tea being the substance.

Finding the poetry in the ordinary is one of Mr McMillan's talents.

But we could all give it a go. Pick the most ordinary thing – and appreciate it anew!

Sunday — June 18

HAVE a friend who has recently joined his church's choir. He joked that his vocal warm-ups got his dog all concerned, but that he was enjoying the music and the companionship of the choir.

I congratulated him, but he said, "It was a comment you made recently that made me believe I could do it."

I was curious as to what the comment had been, but I didn't want to make his moment about me, so I let it go and listened to his thoughts on the hymns they were performing.

But how wonderful to know that a casual comment might cause someone to sing!

"I will be glad and rejoice in thee: I will sing praise to thy name, O thou most High."

Monday — June 19

THEY were celebrating their wedding anniversary on the same day as his grandparents celebrated theirs.

The young wife suggested that their two years were nothing compared to the older couple's 60 years together.

"Ah," Grampa said. "But the first two years are the most difficult."

"If you don't count the next two," Gran added with a smile. "And the two after them. And the two after them . . ."

Marriage is a long series of challenges made worthwhile, hopefully, by an equally long series of overcoming those challenges.

Tuesday — June 20

MICHAEL FAIRLESS (who, in reality, was Margaret Barber), lived her short life in the latter part of the 19th century.

She had 32 years in this world, spending the first half of her curtailed adulthood in charitable work and the second half being cared for, charitably, by wealthy friends.

While being too incapacitated to do much else, she wrote "The Roadmender", which has since gone on to become a spiritual classic.

In a piece called "Out Of The Shadow", she remembered being a girl and watching as Queen Victoria's train passed a level crossing.

"The train slowed down and she caught sight of the gatekeeper's little girl who had climbed the barrier. Such a smile as she gave her! And then I caught a quite startled gesture . . . I thought afterwards that she feared the child might fall. Mother first, then Queen."

A simple little observation, and I sincerely hope her interpretation of it was a true one.

If there is one thing that becomes greatness more than anything else (and something we could do with more of today), it is common humanity.

Wednesday — June 21

THE dam is falling to bits," I overheard someone saying. "The council really should see about fixing it."

Perhaps the individual didn't have my take on it, and even I am not as old as the dam.

More than 100 years ago it was built along the side of a river, narrowing it, raising the level, and feeding it towards the waterwheel that drove the corn mill.

I remember tripping over the ruins of the corn mill when I was a boy at play. I've ventured along the dam through ankle-deep water many a time.

But must "the council" be expected to preserve everything?

There was a time when the earth and the water decided the river's meanderings, and now that we have had our work from it there is a beauty in seeing it slowly return to how it was.

Everything has its season, and the good thing about seasons is that they return.

Thursday — June 22

EIGHT-YEAR-OLD Amelia's appreciation of my neighbour's peonies seemed to go on and on.

"We need to walk on to meet your parents," I reminded her. "You can see the flowers another day."

"Will they be there another day?" she asked.

I looked at those thin stalks and delicate petals. I thought about strong winds and over-excited dogs, or perhaps my neighbour would pick them. So we stood a little longer.

Beauty is often fleeting, so we should really appreciate it in the here and now.

Thanks for the reminder, Amelia.

Friday — June 23

*M*Y flat has got a balcony, and though it's small, you know,
It doesn't hold me back one bit from choosing what to grow.
In spring a tub of daffodils toot golden-trumpet trills,
While pansies, cream and purple hued, shine bright from window-sills.
Sweet strawberries, so plumply red, show summer has begun,
As salad leaves, tomatoes, too, reach up to feel the sun.
A pot of fiery dahlias marks autumn's jubilee,
While even in December's gloom you'll see my Christmas tree.
Who wouldn't want a balcony? It's just the perfect space,
For every day I see it bloom, a smile grows on my face!

Maggie Ingall

Saturday — June 24

I DO love reading inscriptions in old books. This one, written in fountain pen ink with flourishes that made it seem still vibrant, said the book was for "Mr Staneer" from "Reg and Amy".

I doubt any of them are still with us, but along with the book Reg and Amy sent Mr Staneer wishes of "peace and love".

When? In 1944. A year before World War II ended.

Times of war. When better to be sending peace and love?

Sunday — June 25

THERE'S a legend that says that after the crucifixion of Jesus the jasmine flower cried so much that it washed the original pink colour out of its leaves, and they have been pristine white ever since.

The story came to mind when I saw Mark out walking his dog – without Pamela. And when I sat with Elsa, not long after Robert passed.

Grief does change us. It might take some of the colour from our lives. But the jasmine flower is no less beautiful for being white.

Monday — June 26

IN his short story "Sredni Vashtar", Hector Hugh Munro describes Mrs De Ropp as representing "those three-fifths of the world that are necessary and disagreeable and real".

There is a frame of mind that holds that this is an unpleasant world, and that if things are disagreeable then they are somehow more real, more grown up, more true.

It can seem very convincing at times, but don't be taken in.

Years of "study" have convinced me that this is a wonderful world and, personally, I hold with the poet John Keats, who said:

"Beauty is truth, truth beauty – that is all ye know on earth, and all ye need to know."

Tuesday — June 27

HARRY has a friendship plot. It's not a secret plan to get more friends. It's a part of his garden where all the plants were donated by friends, or were cuttings from their gardens.

They are a real mish-mash of types (like Harry's friends) and flower at all different times of the year.

Some are recent gifts, and some came from friends now departed. But Harry can tell you the story of each plant and who it represents.

It's a place of peace for him, and a good suggestion for anyone with a garden.

Wednesday — June 28

THE mesmerising ripples of the river in the sun,
Just trickling on its gentle way, its journey never done.
Bright spikes of yellow iris raise their heads on either side,
And glorious purple foxgloves spread their beauty far and wide.
Sometimes a bobbing moorhen will pop out from the reeds,
A row of chicks behind her like tiny fluffy beads.
There's something very soothing in the music of a stream –
It gently calms the spirit and lets us simply dream.

Eileen Hay

Thursday — June 29

THERE are some homes where, when you visit, you consciously or unconsciously adapt to the mindset of the owner as you step over the threshold because certain things are important to them. Then you shrug it off when you leave.

And there are some homes you visit whose owners welcome your mindset, whatever it might happen to be – because you are important to them.

I will always be happy to visit both types, but I hope that people think my home is the second type.

Friday — June 30

SHE said, "I just wanted to share the experience with you.

"John the window cleaner does the windows, then he cleans my mirrors, and then we generally have a good chat.

"We talk politics, faith, books, films . . . and his take is always upbeat, always positive. He's a regular joy.

"The thing is, he has overcome some very serious medical conditions over the past few years, and now there's one that is only getting worse, but you'd never know it."

The more she told me about him, the more the John-the-window-cleaner experience brightened my day as well.

Some people, I thought, are just like well-cleaned windows. They let the light in better!

July

Saturday — July 1

PICKED up the book "Portrait Of My Mother" by Sir John, the first Viscount Simon, almost prepared to dislike it.

It seemed a vanity project, one upper-class person praising another, surely only bought by people keen to be seen buying it.

I looked him up. He was seen as cold. A story is told of a politician with a first-class rail ticket getting into a third-class compartment to avoid him.

He went up in my estimation when the same story said Simon followed the politician into third-class and sat with him. I read that the proceeds from his biography of his mother went to fight slavery.

His coldness came about after the loss of his much-loved wife. Plus, when he died, his wealth was less than expected, because he was so generous to younger colleagues and the children of friends.

I am a judgemental fool at times. May I learn better before I am too much older.

Sunday — July 2

OUR family home had been lacking a dog's presence for a while. So when our teacher neighbour got herself a golden retriever pup, I volunteered to do the morning walks.

I thought it would be nice to go the old paths, but when I got back out there they were gone. Overgrown. I hadn't realised I had played such a part in keeping those routes open.

My presence, or absence, and those of other walkers, made a difference. The paths could not exist on their own.

So we set off to open up the old ways and make some new paths.

The way we walk through this world will leave paths for others to follow. How better, then, to walk but by following the advice given to Micah in the Old Testament?

Act justly, love mercy, and "walk humbly with thy God".

Monday — July 3

THE Lady Of The House and I were chatting with our friend, Kerry. A working wife and mother, she felt pulled in too many different directions

"Every way I turn just now," she began, "I seem to hit a wall."

My sweetheart had a word with the owner of the café we were sitting in. Then she asked Kerry's children if they would like us to take them to the soft play for a wee while.

The waitress brought coffee and cake. My sweetheart then pointed to the wall beside Kerry's chair and said, "Sometimes walls are for leaning against, while we catch our breath."

I needed all my breath that afternoon!

Tuesday — July 4

HE'S a well-balanced child," his mother told me.

"Glad to hear it," I replied, wondering if two years old wasn't a little young for such psychoanalysis. Then she explained.

"By that I mean, he has a 'wuvwy' stone in each of his hip pockets. So well balanced. And look at that happy swagger as he walks!"

He really was a picture of contentment.

Oh, for a life where we, too, could be as content with the simple things.

Wouldn't that be "wuvwy"?

Wednesday — July 5

WRITING in his book "Country Boy" about his childhood in rural Buckinghamshire before World War I, Richard Hillyer described the impact his fellow villagers had on him.

"They were just run of the mill people, as different, and separate, in their character as run of the mill people usually are, feeling the life in them and enjoying the feel of it. They were basic human nature, and, growing up along with them, you learned how extraordinary that is, and so were free forever of the silly snobbishness of dismissing ordinary people as of no account."

Ordinary people. There really is nothing ordinary about them (us)!

When life gets on top of you, catch your breath with a cuppa and some cake.

Shutterstock.

Thursday — July 6

THE supermarket security guard was quite a talkative guy. But that didn't mean he wasn't also wise.

We struck up a good conversation this day, but he kept interrupting it to say things like "Have a nice day" and "Welcome" to the passing customers.

He turned back to me and said, "The other security guards don't do that – won't do that. They think they have an image to maintain.

"Me? I talk to everyone. They think I'm crazy. But who wants to be that sort of sane?"

Indeed! Not me.

Friday — July 7

IN amongst a box of second-hand books I found a diary.

It had drawings of pirates, dogs and footballers on the pages. It was tatty and worn and dated 1934.

The daily thoughts of a boy in the run-up to World War II would have been fascinating to read, but I didn't pry. I already knew as much as I needed to.

Inside the front cover he had written in a neat hand, "Let me make this day worthwhile – for someone else."

I didn't need to read his diary to know he wanted to be a good man.

In that simple thought he was already halfway there.

Saturday — July 8

I READ that the US Navy has a tradition of baptising babies born to crew members in the ship's bell.

Afterwards, the baby's name is inscribed inside the bell.

It occurred to me that each inscription will, ever so slightly, alter the shape of the bell and the sound it makes.

It may not be noticeable, but the difference is there.

Isn't that how it should be? Each life makes an indelible difference in the world!

Sunday — July 9

DO you ever feel mistreated by others? What's that feeling like? Do you want to get your own back? Do you want to tell your side of the story?

Think for a moment. Do those feelings bring out your best, or does "their" bad behaviour try to drag you to their level?

Isn't that the struggle, after all?

When Hagar was sent into the desert, she found her support in "El Roi", "the God who sees me".

If no-one hears your side of the story, don't worry. God knows!

Monday — July 10

ALISON and I don't meet as often as we'd like because of her busy schedule, so we catch up by e-mail.

Last week her daughter, Maisie, turned two, and Alison's message was packed full of party news.

Then she filled me in on her "real" job.

Her message ended: "I picked Maisie up from nursery after work. Now I need to sign off and go cuddle her again, even though she's sleeping.

"I missed her so much today I was close to tears. It's silly. I can't explain it."

I can, Alison. It's a beautiful thing called a mother's love, and the world's a better place for it.

Tuesday — July 11

I CAUGHT the end of their conversation.

"Oh, isn't that just so sweet?" she remarked.

"No," he replied. "It sounds like made-up nonsense to me!"

He got on his phone to prove his optimistic wife wrong about this thing that was obviously too sweet to be true. And it was true!

"I hope you're not too embarrassed," I whispered.

"Just a little," he replied. "But I do love it when my cynicism is proven wrong!"

Wednesday — July 12

THE musical "Miss Saigon" has many powerful songs in it. None more so than "Bui Doi".

The "bui doi" of the title were children left behind in Vietnam, fathered by American troops. The local name for them was "bui doi" or "the dust of life". They were rejected and counted for nothing.

But when I hear that song, I am reminded of the Joni Mitchell song "Woodstock", in which she sings, "We are stardust, we are golden".

Science tells us that the world, and everything living on it, is composed from the dust of exploding and forming stars.

The dust of life is, indeed, stardust.

I have a difficult time imagining any living person as less than special: tarnished at times, perhaps, but still golden.

Thursday — July 13

MISS WILLMOTT'S GHOST is a flowering plant with the "proper" name of Eryngium giganteum.

Its "common" name comes from Ellen Willmott, a member of the Royal Horticultural Society in the early 1900s.

She was said to be so fond of the plant that she carried its seeds with her and surreptitiously dropped them in the gardens of homes she visited. They would grow months after she left, but would be recognisably her work – something she left behind: her "ghost".

If we would be remembered for anything after we depart this life, we could do worse than choose beauty.

Friday — July 14

AN entry in Great-aunt Louisa's diary tells of her earliest social faux pas – and the response that stayed with her.

When she was four years old, she asked her paternal grandmother if being so awfully old wasn't terribly scary.

Grandmother laughed and sat little Louisa on her knee.

"When I was young," she said, "God was a speck in the distance. Later he was close enough that I could hear him sing. Soon I shall be able to see the love in his face."

A grandparent's words can have a lasting effect.

Shutterstock.

MY neighbours, Bob and Caroline, regularly visit the seashore. They go in all weathers. Often it is how they start their weekend.

Johnny, their eight-year-old son, likes to stand in the shallows, wearing his wellies, to stare out at the sea and the sky.

"I once asked him what he thought about at those times," she told me. "His answer was 'nothing'."

"Did you think that weird?" I asked.

"A little," she replied. "I can't do it. But I'm going to practise."

Some things are so immense that, in their presence, no thoughts are worth the thinking. At times like that, we simply stand and let our souls be refreshed.

Sunday — July 16

IT was a type of clematis with leaves of such a deep purple they were almost black.

"They looked so beautiful, I was sure they had to be artificial," Sadie told me. "But then I told myself off for even thinking that!"

"Why?" I asked.

"Because there's nothing manmade that doesn't have a more beautiful equivalent in God's creation!" she replied.

It started me wondering if I knew of something to prove Sadie wrong. I'm still wondering!

Monday — July 17

WORRIED he would die young, H.G. Wells compiled a book, called "'42 to '44", on all that was important to him. It was a large book and prohibitively expensive.

Later he declared that all of that work could "fall into oblivion". Sure he only had months left, he wrote down the things that really mattered to him. This volume, called "A Mind At The End Of Its Tether", is 34 pages long.

Many of us have so much to say about so many things. But when it comes down to it, only a few things really matter. The younger we are when we realise what they are, the better.

Tuesday — July 18

H E asked for help again. I had the feeling that I was being taken advantage of. What to do?

"Who would you be doing it for?" the voice in my head asked. "For you? Or a greater good? Perhaps he is thankful, but has an unfortunate way of showing it. Imagine he really needed this, but your suspicions prevented you from helping."

"But," I objected (to myself), "he might be taking advantage!"

"Answer me this," the voice persisted. "Have you been given more in this life than you ever could give? Aren't you taking advantage?"

It annoys me, on a regular basis, how good at arguing that voice in my head is.

I helped. He might not have needed it, but he might. The loss, if it was a loss, won't ever outweigh my gratitude

If it turns out I was wrong and my pride takes a hit – that's no bad thing, either.

Wednesday — July 19

A WHEEL came off her scooter on the path behind our house. Because I was only reading a book with my eyes closed, she asked me for help.

I set to work with a spanner and restored her scooting ability in minutes.

She seemed impressed and asked if I knew lots of things.

I confessed to knowing a thing or two, so she tested me with the subtraction sums she had been learning at school.

Thankfully, my answers only lifted me up in her estimation.

"But," she asked, "can you scratch your ear with your toes?"

Lest she ask me to prove that I could, I quickly confessed that I couldn't.

She seemed concerned.

"Never mind. When you are too stiff and old to do all the things you know how to, and when I know how to do a few more things, I shall help you like you helped me."

I told her I would very much appreciate that.

I was smiling, but I found myself surprisingly sincere.

I LOVE it when the sun shines down –
It lifts the heart and smooths the frown;
It drives away the cold and rain
To coax us out of doors again.

And up there, in the azure sky,
I see the swifts and swallows fly,
Whilst other birds, now, all day long
Sound out their sweet, long summer song.

The gardens, parks and country lanes
Flourish as the sun retains
Its welcome hold upon the land,
Spreading warmth, like God had planned.

John Darley

IT seemed an odd thing to say, but when our dear friend Mary speaks, I am used to thinking twice.

I'd mentioned what a lovely day it was.

"I never judge a day by the weather," she said. "I judge it by the people in it. This would have been a lesser day if I hadn't met you."

I conceded the point and left with a new take on what makes a good day.

LEAVING the house, Morag noticed the banner and balloons stuck to her neighbour's door. Popping in, Morag asked which birthday it was.

"Tell me what age you'd be," Annie replied, "if there were no calendars or dates of birth."

In Morag's mind she was still young, her energy never-ending, her skin was smooth, and her heart still full of hope for the future.

As she started to reply, Annie held a finger to her lips.

"Me, too," she said.

GUNNER MITCHELL was a POW on the infamous bridge over the River Kwai during World War II. After his liberation, the first thing he did was write to his sweetheart.

Where he assured her that he would be home soon, the handwriting gets wobbly. Then he added: "Home. What a wonderful word."

Home. A wonderful concept in this world. How much more so will it be in the next?

THE trees stood, one, two, three, descending a steep bank. The top tree was the most exposed to the wind.

I remember the day it fell. The tree beneath caught it, but the effort lifted its roots a little. The third tree steadied them both.

That was five years ago. They stood, intertwined, for a while, presumably putting down new roots, firming the bank and securing themselves.

Today I noticed there was blue sky between the three of them. All were standing independently.

Sometimes all we need is a friend to catch us when we fall and take the strain while we recover.

Then we can grow towards the sun again.

FRANCIS KILVERT was an English clergyman who lived in the West Midlands in the mid to late 1800s.

Never famous in his lifetime, his diaries of rural life found a readership when they were published after his death.

"It is a fine thing to be out on the hills alone," he wrote. "A man can hardly be a beast or a fool alone on a great mountain."

It needn't be a great mountain, but it is a useful exercise to occasionally find yourself outside, away from the hubbub every once in a while. Then a person can really take stock of themselves – away from what others think.

Wednesday — July 26

I WATCHED a crow and a hawk rise from some dew-bedecked scrubland into a sapphire sky.

They fought a spiralling duel across the piercing morning sun, before disappearing into the silhouetted woods. Moments later, they emerged, apparently unscathed, and flew off in different directions.

It occurred to me that the hawk had made all the noise, and each talon-centred circle they had carved across the sky took them both a little further away from whatever the crow had been protecting.

Well done, Mr Crow. Often our best work is done quietly and in little steps.

Thursday — July 27

THE picture was of three young women enjoying themselves at the theatre.

One of them – a friend – had posted it on social media just before curtain-up. All three looked excited and delighted.

But beneath the sleeve of the pretty top one of them was wearing, I could see the edge of the bandage that protected her PICC line.

This "valve" helped deliver the strong medications she needed.

Looking at the photo, I thought of the value of a good night out in maintaining our spirits and (I believe) our health.

It reminded me of the ancient truth – that we never know the battles the person next to us might be fighting.

Love one another. Just in case.

Friday — July 28

THE graffiti artist credited the words on the wall to the Persian poet Rumi. They said, "Walk out of your house like a shepherd."

I didn't get it at first. Then I wondered, "What does a shepherd do when he or she walks out of the house?"

The answer that came back was, "They look for their flock, and spend the rest of the day taking care of them."

To anyone who doesn't think that's a fine way to spend the day, can I just say, "Baaa!"

Saturday — July 29

I **STOOD** in the queue while the man ahead of me regaled the checkout operator with the government's short-comings and told her, in detail, what policies they should put in place.

When he'd finished bagging his shopping and walked on, I remarked, "You were very patient there."

"I had nowhere else to go," she replied. "He obviously needed to let it all out, so I thought I might as well be nice about it."

I lifted my shopping into the trolley and said I'd see her next time.

She lifted a bar of chocolate from the bagging area.

"You forgot this."

"It has nowhere else to go," I replied. "You may as well be nice to it."

Sunday — July 30

W **HEN** I visited Rab's house there was an Etch A Sketch on the table.

"Normally, I would have tidied it away," he said. "But I can't help looking at it."

There were two handprints drawn in outline on the screen.

The bigger one, I guessed, was Rab's. The smaller one, which fitted completely inside the palm of Rab's hand, belonged to his two-year-old grandson.

"It's strange," he said. "This picture reminds me I won't always be here, but that through my children and grandchildren I will live on."

God, of course, has all of that (dare I say it?) in hand.

Monday — July 31

I **MET** Harry and Jim in the street. They had been for a coffee.

"What did you talk about?" I asked.

"Man stuff!" Harry replied gruffly.

Jim nodded his head in firm agreement

"We talked about our wives and how lucky we are to have them!"

The best sort of man stuff!

August

Tuesday — August 1

THE month of August is named after the Roman emperor Augustus Caesar. His 40 years in power were a high point for the Roman Empire, with literature and the arts flourishing during a time of relative peace.

The empire expanded hugely under his rule and he supervised the rebuilding of much of Rome itself.

It is said of him that he found Rome made of brick and left it made of marble.

Most of us will never wield anything like that amount of power, but making a difference for the better doesn't need to be about wealth or power.

The transition from brick to marble intrigues me, though, and I have to wonder: this August, what might we (each of us), for 31 days, take and make better?

Wednesday — August 2

ELIAS is almost eight years old. His teacher set the class the exercise of writing a list of their best attributes.

Well, he rattled his off!

Then he looked around and saw Jack, who hadn't written anything on his list and was staring into space.

He went over and told the boy six things he liked about him and encouraged him to write them down.

"My mum and dad are always telling me what I'm good at," he told me later. "I guess Jack's parents have been too busy, so I did it for them."

Barnabas (whose name meant "son of encouragement") has long been my favourite disciple from the Bible stories. He didn't invent encouragement, but he embodied it.

It's nice to see his tradition live on in Elias.

Making a difference doesn't have to be about wealth and power.

Thursday — August 3

OUR neighbours have a variety of bird feeders in their back garden.

I'm sure the local bird population appreciate them very much, but the birds aren't the only ones.

Every time it rains (when the birds are sheltering elsewhere), their cat (who hates getting wet) climbs up the pole and squeezes itself into the bird house!

If we are offering shelter, then we offer just that. Shelter.

We can't be too fussy about who needs it!

Friday — August 4

THE Battle of Copenhagen in 1807 pretty much destroyed the Danish navy.

The country's response, according to popular legend, was to plant 90,000 oak trees.

When the trees matured, they would be used to build the next fleet of mighty wooden ships.

An oak tree can take 200 years to mature. Ships and navies have changed dramatically since then.

I doubt those oaks will ever sail to war, but think of the good they have been doing, day in and day out, ever since they were planted!

Saturday — August 5

THIS man had been writing and speaking about bullying. Gordon couldn't believe it.

He took his courage in both hands and asked if the man remembered being Gordon's tutor at college – and bullying him!

There was an awkward silence. Then the man said, "I do. And I'm sorry. Thinking about those times is what made me want to be better, and try to prevent it from happening again elsewhere."

I asked Gordon how he felt about that, and he recited this quote attributed to the great Russian writer Dostoevsky.

"A fool who's admitted he is a fool is a fool no more!"

Sunday — August 6

WE all know the commandment "Thou shalt not take the name of the Lord thy God in vain."

I imagine most people think this involves swearing and the like.

But there's a story of a church in the 1800s that suffered a schism over a chicken leg at a picnic.

One man said the Lord wanted him to have it. The other man said the Lord didn't care, but he wanted it.

The argument spread and temporarily split the church.

Is this, perhaps, the sort of casual usage – and the assumption that God only cares for us – the "in vain" that the commandment had in mind?

God is love. If we use his name, let it always be used in love.

Monday — August 7

IN days gone by, a hunted person could claim sanctuary at Durham Cathedral by grasping hold of the knocker on the main door.

There is a window above the door where a monk would sit to watch out for sanctuary seekers and open the door for them.

I often wondered what doubts and fears went through the monks' minds when deciding who they would hurry down to help – or if they would.

I wonder if I would want a man like me at that window, if I was also the one being chased!

Tuesday — August 8

AS Julie's neighbour's macular degeneration grew worse, she took on the role of a seeing-eye companion.

The two of them would walk arm in arm around the neighbourhood, with Julie describing what she saw.

At first it was awkward and she couldn't find much to say, but a few months down the line she realised she'd hardly stopped talking.

Her neighbour has gone on ahead now, but Julie often thinks about her, and thanks her for teaching her how to see.

Wednesday — August 9

THE story is true, but let's keep it to basics, because the details are too much.

He was terminally ill. She was beside him in a park, describing the scene and the light of the sun across the duck pond.

She was determined that he would experience as much as possible in the time he had left. Then she asked him, if he could do anything, what would he choose?

After a moment's consideration, he whispered, "Here. This."

The wisdom from this, the reason I share it, is that this moment is all we ever have. Make it beautiful.

Thursday — August 10

IT might have happened or it might be a myth. Either way, it is a powerful lesson if we take it.

Greek mathematician Euclid is said to have enraged his brother about something or other.

"May I die if I am not revenged on you at one time or another!" his furious brother shouted.

Euclid's response was more gentle.

"And may I die if I do not soften you with my kindness and make you love me as well as ever."

I do know of people who could stubbornly resist such a loving, self-sacrificing response. But not for long.

Friday — August 11

SOMEONE had annoyed Harry and he fumed all night. Next morning, he set out, determined to continue the argument.

He hadn't closed the gate behind him before Sarah stopped to say how lovely his garden looked. Then he met Andy, who wanted to thank him for his help in a time of need.

Approaching the scene of yesterday's conflict, Harry's mood had softened. Maybe I'll just be nice instead, he thought. And he was.

Sarah and Andy never knew the explosion they defused simply by setting a fine example.

Saturday — August 12

I CAN'T paint. I can't sculpt. I couldn't throw a pot to save myself. But I take comfort from the words of Henry Thoreau.

"It is far more glorious to carve and paint the very atmosphere and medium through which we look, which morally we can do. To affect the quality of the day, that is the highest of arts."

There's no special training required, and you save a fortune on materials!

Whether a sketch or a masterpiece, make this day your own work of art.

Sunday — August 13

A ROUGH sleeper asked Danni the time.

"Almost nine," she replied. "The church service is about to start."

"I've thought about going in," the woman said, "but I don't think I'd be welcome."

"If they let Jesus in," Danni said, "they'll let anyone in."

Some worshippers weren't happy about the woman sitting near them, so Danni said, "Come sit with me."

After the service, the woman hugged Danni and left.

"It's not exactly a parable," Danni told me.

Isn't it? I had to think hard to make sure there wasn't something just like that in the New Testament.

Monday — August 14

WHAT can ordinary people do to reverse the effects of industrialisation or climate change?

Jia Haixia and Jia Wenqi live in a village in northern China that is prone to flooding. They decided to plant as many trees as they could, to soak up water and prevent the soil from eroding.

One is blind and one has no arms, but it is estimated that they have planted between 10,000 and 13,000 trees.

They can work because they work together, and they are making a difference.

Tuesday — August 15

BERNIE felt a little out his depth after a morning's vocational training, so he slipped away to an overgrown lot, thinking he could have a sandwich in peace.

Walking through the long grass, he became aware of a young fox ahead of him.

It was completely focused on stalking a butterfly.

Bernie froze, watching the fox practise its stealthy moves until the butterfly, unhurriedly, fluttered out of reach.

He returned, smiling, after lunch, knowing that he wasn't the only one on vocational training this day.

The fox cub would get the hang of it – and so would he!

Wednesday — August 16

HE runs a second-hand bookshop in Melrose. One day, a man spent an hour browsing, then headed towards the door without buying anything.

Then he turned and handed my friend a rather large banknote.

"You have almost every book I read as a child in here. I couldn't buy one or I would have had to buy them all.

"Simply being here, and seeing them, has taken fifty years off me. The money is my thanks to you. Keep it or put it in the charity tin; I just felt the experience was worth it."

Some experiences we can never buy, but that doesn't mean we shouldn't appreciate them all the same.

Thursday — August 17

LUCY CLIFFORD was a novelist and journalist in the late 19th and early 20th century. She penned some words on goodness that bear thinking about even now.

"Consider this," she wrote. "Your goodness is of no use if you are not good to others . . . The good of goodness is that you can wrap others inside it. It ought to be like a big cloak that you have on a cold night, while the shivering person next to you has none. If you don't make use of your goodness, what is the good of it?"

Friday — August 18

JUST over the horizon is the promise of intent,
A chance to be the best you can in this new day just sent.
To make new friends or heal old wounds, it's really up to you,
To keep love in your heart and hands, in everything you do.
A promise kept, a promise made, do your actions leave you
pleased?
To know that when the hours slip by the day's been truly seized,
To live each moment fully, and with your head held high,
No better than your fellow man, nor not so much awry.
Just over the horizon, yet close within your reach,
Your footprint's cast and left from the lessons that you teach.
When you keep moving forward, acquiring wisdom every day,
You will soar over the horizon in your unique and precious way.

Elizabeth McGinty

Saturday — August 19

HAVE you ever felt daunted by the size of the tasks ahead of you? I suggest you don't look at all the work to be done, just make a beginning! Beginnings are wonderful things.

In his "Life Thoughts", Henry Ward Beecher wrote, "The beginning is the promise of the end.

"The seed always whispers 'oak', though it is going into the ground acorn. I am sure that the first little blades of wheat are just as pleasant to the farmer's eye as the whole field waving with grain."

Sunday — August 20

PEOPLE sometimes ask what my favourite Bible verse is. I say I have four favourite Bible words instead – "It is the Lord", from when John and Peter see the risen Christ on the shore while they are fishing, but it speaks to me of so much more.

If they ask me to explain, I might take them outside, show them the world, then expand those four words a little.

"It is all the Lord."

May we live lives of plenty.

Monday — August 21

THERE'S a definition of "plenty" often attributed to American statesman Benjamin Franklin.

He gave the boy a shiny red apple almost as big as his hand. The boy received it happily.

He gave the boy another apple. The boy was delighted.

He then gave the boy a third apple.

No matter how hard he tried, the boy couldn't hold these three large apples in his hands, and in the end he dropped all three and burst out crying.

One apple was a good thing. Two were plenty. Beyond that . . .

May we live lives of plenty, and never want for more!

Tuesday — August 22

MAKE a little memory,
Something fine each day.
Store it in your memory bank
And some day it will pay
The most amazing dividends
When your stocks are low –
For the interest that your memories make
Will grow, and grow, and grow.

Pamela Blood

Wednesday — August 23

HE gets excited every time he sees someone doing this," the mother said. "I think it is what he wants to do when he grows up."

The worker, wet, dirty and weary, lifted himself out of the trench he had dug under the town-centre slabbing and fist-bumped the two-year-old.

"Good for you, little man. You can come and work with me. I'll save you a shovel."

Watching from the sidelines, I couldn't tell whose day had been made happier by the encounter.

Thursday — August 24

THE role of a GP has changed a lot, but they still do marvellous work.

I recalled a local doctor, who would always come out to see sick children, no matter the time of day or night, and a friend suggested I might be remembering "through rose-tinted glasses."

The son of Dr Robert Lynch happened to be in our company at the time.

"We would know if Dad had been called out in the night," he said, "if at breakfast we could see his pyjama legs peeking out from under his suit trousers."

God bless the generations of doctors who went – and go – the extra mile to take care of us.

Friday — August 25

WHAT is it with golden retrievers and muddy puddles?" he asked as his pet semi-submerged itself.

I didn't know.

It's been my experience that every dog big enough to enjoy it will play in mud or splash in puddles whenever they can.

We think more of it with fair-furred dogs than we do with darker-furred dogs because it shows up more. We think of the yellow or white coats as prettier, perhaps more delicate.

But the dog isn't aware of our preconceptions.

Saturday — August 26

IT is so tempting to "give as good as you got" when someone does us a bad turn, and this can often be our biggest struggle.

The "Good Emperor" and philosopher Marcus Aurelius had this suggestion on how we ought to respond whenever we are wronged.

"The best sort of revenge is not to be like him who did the injury."

If it was wrong of them, it will be just as wrong of us.

Rise up. Give better in return. Be better in return.

Sunday — August 27

IT was a church-run playgroup, but it was open to the whole community.

I sat by the side and watched mums, grandparents and children from all different backgrounds.

They were playing, chatting, learning to share and making new friends. It was beautiful.

I couldn't help thinking of all the places in the world where such simple happiness and contentment wouldn't be possible because of war, division, poverty and other such unpleasant things.

I understood, in a new way, the phrase from the Beatitudes, "Blessed are the peacemakers."

Monday — August 28

TODAY, nothing much happened. And it was lovely! Which is why the ancient Chinese expression "May you live in interesting times" is not always a blessing.

Interesting times – the times studied by historians – tend to be marked by war, political upheaval or natural disasters.

Historians rarely study the days where people just got on, raised their families, ate a good breakfast, visited their neighbours and did someone a good turn.

I'll take one of those uninteresting days as often as I can get them.

Tuesday — August 29

THE book was a century old with a soft leather cover. Once there had been a ribbon to mark the reader's place.

The parts of the ribbon that had emerged from the binding at the top of the book, and where it had hung out the bottom of the book had frayed away.

Between the pages, however, the rest of the ribbon was held, protected and surrounded by words of wisdom.

Books, bless them, have often done the same for me in "fraying" times.

A little piece of canine heaven – the muddy puddle!

Wednesday — August 30

SHE was pleased with herself and, truthfully, it was a little wicked of him.

The young scholar had finally, and correctly, recited her 12 times table.

"And twelve times twelve is one hundred and forty-four!" she told her grandparents.

"Well done," the old man replied. "Now, what is thirteen times thirteen?

"There's no such thing!" the girl, who was used to his nonsense, responded.

"Thereafter began the bigger lesson," he told me.

"Not to listen to Grampa?" I suggested.

"Perhaps," he replied, laughing. "But also that there is always more to learn."

Thursday — August 31

IT'S the oft-repeated tale of an old sea-dog, so it might be true.

His boat's engine ran into some technical difficulty and failed, so he hoisted the sail and waited for a breeze.

Unfortunately, when the breeze came, it was in the form of a dreadful storm.

He was forced to pull the sails down before they ripped, and batten down the hatches.

It was a fierce storm.

Hour after hour, the wind grew stronger and the waves grew higher.

His original notion that he would simply manage to ride it out eventually paled into acceptance that this storm might be the end of him.

Then he felt what he thought must be a sand bar beneath the keel of the boat.

It wasn't that – it was the shore.

The very waves he had felt sure would drive him down had actually been driving him home!

September

Friday — September 1

THE young bulls were having fun in the field. They butted heads, ran rings around each other, kicked their hind legs out, and sometimes jumped up off all four hooves at the one time.

"Look at them gambolling," I said to my sweetheart.

"Just like lambs in springtime," she replied.

It crossed my mind to wonder why we always associate the word "gambolling" with lambs. Because they do it so well?

The bulls had their own version of it and seemed to enjoy it nonetheless. So could we, if we wanted to.

The idea that one way of behaving is reserved for certain creatures, or types of people, is far too restrictive in my opinion.

If any of us feel like having a good gambol, we should go for it!

Saturday — September 2

IT was an after-church lunch.

"You know the old woman who lives in the bushes in the car park behind the bank?" someone asked. They all said they did, except me.

They explained that she was homeless, that she had built a sleeping space from scraps of wood and covered it with old carpet. She lived there with her cats.

I asked if anyone had visited her. They were sure someone must have, but, no, not them.

I bought some cat food and went to see how I could help.

When I arrived, the space had been cleared, but I could see how the bushes had grown around some sort of shelter. There was a pet's food bowl in the dirt.

What happened to her, I do not know. I was too late to help.

How much more would it have bothered me to have known about her and not tried?

Sunday — September 3

IT was a quote attributed to the 19th-century English preacher F.W. Robertson that reminded me of David.

The quote was: "You must love in order to understand love."

David had been a critic of faith for a long time. He just couldn't leave the subject alone.

Deciding he had complained about it for long enough, the only thing left was to try living as if it were true and see how it worked.

He has been a man of solid faith for 20 years now.

Love and faith? You need to experience them to come close to understanding their wonders!

Monday — September 4

IN the old days, James would have been known as a "character". Now, describing how he relates to the world, he is diagnosed as having a few different syndromes.

He described it to me like this.

"Some see the world through a telescope, and some see the world through a kaleidoscope.

"The second way can be confusing, but it is also fascinating, in a way worth the confusion. As for the first way – you tell me."

"Maybe," I replied, "the telescope looks ahead and provides focus."

"Those are important, too," James allowed. "We need both ways."

I'd say that's the best way to look at the world.

Tuesday — September 5

PHILLIPS BROOKS, the American preacher, once said, "Find your purpose and fling your life out into it."

I remember talking to an old countryman about crossing fast-flowing streams out on the hills. He told me he always flung his coat across first.

I asked him how that helped.

"Well, I only got one coat! You see?" he replied.

Commitment! That's the key.

Wednesday — September 6

IT'S hard to hold on to your troubles
When you walk all alone on the shore,
For the waves seem to whisper their comfort
As they've done for millennia before.
While the sky is so wide and unending
That anxieties shrink into place,
And the breeze that has travelled the oceans
Fills our hearts with new courage and grace,
May the gifts given freely by nature
Ever stay with us all, day by day,
And the solace and peace of their presence
Sustain us, each one, on our way.

Maggie Ingall

Thursday — September 7

IS there anything more innately kind and generous than those little free libraries that people put up in their gardens or their neighbourhoods, where passers-by can leave or borrow books?

Nicola thinks she found something that was.

Inside one of those donated books was a postcard that read: "You are beautiful. Have a blessed day."

And there was a quote from the American writer Garrison Keillor that read: "A book is a gift you can open again and again."

Kindness upon kindness. Generosity upon generosity.

Friday — September 8

I LIKED this comparison between people and torches: all of our batteries run low from time to time!

Torches use AA batteries, or AAA, or C or D.

We can't physically change people's power packs, but when their light is low we can give them AA, or attention and affection; AAA, or attention and affection with acceptance; C for compassion; or D for direction.

If those don't work, we can sit with them and be a light in their darkness until they feel a bit brighter.

Saturday — September 9

I'VE often heard the advice that resentment is like holding a hot coal and expecting someone else to get their fingers burned.

Today, I heard another, similar, piece of wisdom.

"Anger is the punishment we give ourselves for someone else's mistake."

Neither anger nor resentment are worth the space they occupy in our minds, or the damage they do while there. Both have more positive alternatives.

We should value ourselves as more than just carriers of someone else's wrongs.

Forgive or forget (not easy, but possible). Then carry on living our lives!

Sunday — September 10

ADELAIDE PROCTER was Queen Victoria's favourite poet, second only in demand to Alfred, Lord Tennyson.

Her poems focused on the social issues of the downtrodden and the effects of war.

Modern readers may say this verse was about post-traumatic stress disorder, but it also speaks to how we see our fellow human beings.

"Judge not; the working of his brain and of his heart thou canst not see; What looks to thy dim eyes a stain, in God's pure light may only be a scar brought from some well-won field, where thou wouldst only faint and yield."

Until we know the battle fought, as God does, be kind!

Monday — September 11

DRIVERS in Macau use the left-hand side of the road, but drivers in neighbouring China use the right-hand side.

The Lotus Bridge, which connects the two, splits the road in two, spins it through a roundabout system, and reunites it on the other side so that drivers who were on the left are now on the right.

Different ways can, with a little thought and care, get along side by side!

Tuesday — September 12

I HAD work to do. Instead, I watched my neighbour's dog chase her tail until she caught it!

Not content with that, she wrestled with it for the next 10 minutes. I wondered what a victory in that tail tug-of-war would be!

Then I thought about how often we spend time fighting with ourselves, to no real purpose, spinning in circles, getting nowhere.

I threw her a treat for a distraction. Then I fetched myself a cuppa and a chocolate biscuit, and settled down to that work.

Wednesday — September 13

S OMETIMES it seems like everything has changed and become more high-tech! But some things haven't changed in a long time.

Walking through a new car park, I noticed two red buckets, full of sand and hung on hooks.

The same sort of fire buckets we had at school when I was young; the same fire-dousing method they put to good use during World War II!

Sand spreads easily, it smothers just about every sort of flame, and isn't even a little flammable.

Why change what has almost always worked?

If we are lucky, we have people like that in our lives. Reliable, then, now, and always.

The kind of friends we need never change!

Thursday — September 14

T HE poet William Wordsworth claims he delighted in this thing when he was a child, and also when he was a young man.

He wrote, in his poem "My Heart Leaps Up", that if he no longer delighted in it as an old man, then he had probably lived too long.

What was this marvellous thing, worth enjoying for a whole life?

A rainbow!

Wordsworth would surely have agreed with fellow poet John Keats, who wrote, "A thing of beauty is a joy for ever."

THE world is an awful place, according to some. It's not like it was when we were young. Well . . . no. Nor should it be.

While we insist we aren't looking at the past through rose-tinted glasses, it's often the case.

How we view the state of the world is a subjective, personal thing.

Thomas Carlyle, the Scottish essayist, had a useful take on the matter.

"Such is the world," he wrote. "Understand it, despise it, love it; cheerfully hold on thy way through it with thine eyes on higher lodestars."

Perhaps if we focused more on our guiding principles, the things that matter most to us – and making them "higher" and finer – then the world could get on with being its natural, wonderful self.

MARY has an expression for when someone puts a lot of effort in but fails to win a prize.

"He did his poor best," she'll say.

Most of our bests are poor efforts compared to those with more resources or more natural ability. That's just life.

But imagine if poor bests were recognised – a fourth step on the winners' podium, if you like, for the ones who did the most with what they had!

I ASKED Hugh, a pastor, what he thought of the afterlife.

"Different traditions tell you different things," he said. "But I don't know.

"I do know, however, exactly what happens when you forgive someone. When you work to improve your neighbourhood.

"When you teach your kids to accept people different from them. When you make the table more accessible for everyone . . ."

He sticks with what he knows, takes the rest on trust, and is, in my opinion, a better pastor – and person – because of it.

How we view the
world is personal to us.

125

Monday — September 18

THE art critic John Ruskin took a charitable view of humanity, believing that "Very few people really mean to do wrong – in a deep sense, none. They only don't know what they are about."

Having been annoyed by more people than usual this morning, I was about to disagree. Then I thought that maybe he meant me – in which case, I welcomed his charity!

What should those who do know what they are about do about that situation?

Keep on showing the better, kinder example, so that others may learn.

Tuesday — September 19

LIZ has been dealing with a difficult situation for some years now. People keep urging her to quit, to walk away, but she is of the opinion that we should never judge a journey until we reach our destination.

By way of explanation, a friend of hers, a keen hillwalker, said:

"Ninety-nine point nine per cent of every ascent of any hill is spent looking at the grass or the rocks directly in front of you. Very uninspiring and definitely not worth the trip. But then you reach the summit and everything changes!"

If you have a good destination in mind, no matter how arduous the journey is, keep going.

It's the last few steps that make all the others worthwhile.

Wednesday — September 20

MIRIAM was the sister of Moses – the one who hid the baby boy in the reeds and ensured his survival.

I have heard that Jewish tradition credits her goodness with the fact that sources of water were always to be found when, as an adult, Moses led his people through the desert.

Siblings at their best are like that – always a help in our times of need. If they aren't, for whatever reason, you can be sure that a part of them very much wants to be!

Thursday — September 21

I HEAR that market traders in Indonesia are in the habit of advertising their goods as "the same but different".

What they mean is that you might find whatever they are selling at another stall, but their goods are somehow superior, you will get a better deal, or the experience will be a happier one.

"The same but different" is also a way to live a life. We might be like everyone else, but hold ourselves to a higher standard in something, be it in faith, honesty, integrity or whatever.

What it is that makes you different is for you to decide. Make it something good, something beneficial, and then make the very best you can out of it.

Be the same – but different!

Friday — September 22

PEOPLE have asked me if I don't find the noise of the nearby school distracting. Children at play? I could listen to that all day.

Today I was hanging a washing on the line and, in the distance, a child was singing a song from "Willy Wonka And The Chocolate Factory".

"Come with me," the happy voice sang, "and you'll be, in a world of pure imagination!"

I closed my eyes in the morning sunshine and imagined being back at primary school.

Somehow, I felt much more youthful for the rest of the day.

Saturday — September 23

WORDSWORTH thought that every human being had a desire to do some good for others.

Even "the poorest poor" longed for those moments when they could be "the dealers out of some small blessings" to "such as needed kindness."

He thought this for one simple reason – "That we have all of us one human heart."

Wouldn't it be nice to think that were true?

Sunday — September 24

AEROPLANES fly above the clouds for obvious reasons. If only it were as straightforward for people!

Unlike aeroplanes, we tend to be victims of clouds, be they meteorological or psychological in nature.

When you are looking down from a plane window, all you can see for seemingly endless miles are the brilliantly white, marshmallow-like clouds.

If you look through the breaks in the cloud, you might see the darker underbelly of the clouds, the rain falling from them and the shadows they cast.

You can imagine the people underneath them being pretty miserable. I'm sure we've all experienced a dark, cloudy day.

But it doesn't have to be that way. Consider it this way instead.

The sun is actually still shining brightly through the majority of the sky. There's just some low-level, insubstantial stuff getting in the way.

On the dull days, take the higher view.

God's love is still most of the sky. We just need, somehow, to blow away those clouds.

Monday — September 25

THERE was an Irish woman who lived in the village where I grew up.

More than a few of us children were glad, and lucky enough, to call her Granny Maggie.

Many a time, when an adult did something wrong, she would say, "They're more to be pitied than scorned!"

She would use the expression for people she thought genuinely didn't know any better, or couldn't do any better.

And, all the while, other adults would settle for anger!

Granny Maggie's pity was real.

It closed no doors, and always allowed for better later.

In international and inter-personal matters, could we say we have tried scorn for long enough?

The sun is always shining somewhere.

Tuesday — September 26

I **HAVE** long known about, and admired, the Japanese art of kintsugi, where broken pottery is mended with seams of gold.

Now, it seems, there is an artist in the French city of Lyon who fixes holes in the concrete and tarmac of the roads, pavements and walls by filling them with brightly coloured mosaic tiles.

When it comes to ways to fix or beautify the physical world we live in, it's beginning to seem like our imagination is the only limit.

It might be an idea to wonder what we can do with our little corner of it.

Now that I mention it, someone did knit a hat for a letter-box in our town recently . . .

Wednesday — September 27

THE problem was a mix-up with a hotel booking.

The woman needing assistance, Julie, sounded very Welsh. I knew that the two women staffing the reception desk spoke with French and Indian accents. They were having a difficult day.

As Julie handed over her paperwork, a little bling was noticed and all three women joined together in admiration of her nail art and the skill of the nail technician who did them.

Then, having established a happy common ground, they all got on with dealing with the problem and a positive outcome was achieved.

You see what a little beauty can add to the mix?

Thursday — September 28

ONE of the chief delights of an ordinary unplanned day is never knowing what it might bring!

I thought of this as I read a quote in a hundred-year-old book. The words were credited only to "Miss Palmer".

"We seldom meet with joy and delight by appointment, but unexpectedly they smile on us their sudden welcome round some old corner of life."

Let us meet each day prepared – if that is even possible – for unexpected joy.

Friday — September 29

IN 1803, the Romantic writers William and Dorothy Wordsworth and Samuel Taylor Coleridge went on a famous tour through Scotland.

In part, the journey was also a tribute to Robert Burns, whose poetic works they all admired.

Of course, you get to know people better than ever when you journey with them.

Coleridge's notes, written after a day's ride along the Nithsdale Valley, recorded these thoughts on that matter.

"I went to sleep after dinner and reflected how little there was in this world that would compensate for the loss or diminishment of the love of such that truly love us.

"And what had calculators vanity and selfishness prove to be in the long run."

We might have a high or low esteem of ourselves, but those who truly know us will have a much more honest measure of our character, having seen us in various circumstances.

If they love us still, having seen us at our best and our worst, then that love should be valued beyond all things.

Saturday — September 30

*I**LOVE** this gentle hour, as nature settles to her sleep –*
Daylight shaking hands with dusk, a sign that it will keep
Its promise to bring sunrise once again to morning skies –
A gift from the creator, all powerful, all wise.

While high above the birds sing a finale clear and bold,
One last ray of setting sun turns nearby trees to gold.
Around me everything is stilled in this day's closing hour,
Enfolding safe its memories, like petals on a flower.

Soon, so soon, dark velvet cloak of night will bring us rest,
Stars are waiting in the wings to shine their very best,
But this brief intermission is a blessing, ours to keep
And cherish in the heart, as nature settles to her sleep.

Marian Cleworth

October

THE negative things in life have a fascination for people, as we feel our survival might depend on us knowing about them.

That's not the case. The world is an overwhelmingly good and kind place. We could see that more clearly if we got into the habit of looking for it, and not for the other stuff.

Like all habits, it takes practice.

As St Paul advised in his letter to the Philippians: "Whatsoever things are true, whatsoever things are honest, whatsoever things are just, whatsoever things are pure, whatsoever things are lovely, whatsoever things are of good report; if there be any virtue and if there be any praise, think on these things."

You won't be short of things to think about!

THE skies resound with ordered flocks
En route to winter homes,
While in the brown and empty fields
A scarecrow stands alone.
The crops are safely gathered in
And we can now rejoice.
It's time to sing familiar hymns –
In thanks we raise our voice,
For all the work the farmers do
Their faithful toil and care,
With factories and delivery teams
Who also do their share,
So markets, bakeries and shops –
Far more than we could name –
Can keep us all supplied with food
Come sunshine or come rain.

Laura Tapper

Tuesday — October 3

THE words of the Canadian national anthem might not be too well known in the UK, but as Ronald sat looking out of a hotel window in Toronto, he found he could sing them word for word.

"I'd never been in Canada before," Ronald told me afterwards. "When I was twelve, I got a Dansette record player, but I had no records to play on it.

"My auntie, who had emigrated when I was a baby, sent me an LP of Canadian songs. 'O Canada' was the first track I ever played.

"She's passed on now and I'm sixty-five. But that's how long a kindness can last."

At least!

Wednesday — October 4

THERE'S a quote attributed to Benjamin Franklin that goes, "I would see clearly, near or far."

I don't know if that genius of a man was referring to spectacles or telescopes, or some other sort of lens, but I suspect he had something more profound in mind.

For myself, whether we are talking about international affairs or how my nearest and dearest are feeling, I would ask something similar.

That I see clearly. That I understand.

Thursday — October 5

PAT is an amateur wildlife photographer. She set out one day in the hope of getting some shots of rarely seen bearded tits.

Arriving at the riverside, she was horrified to see two individuals netting the birds. Her first instinct was to stop them or call the police.

It turned out they were from a bird protection charity, ringing the birds to track them and help protect them.

They offered Pat a closer look, and she got some beautiful photos.

People, and situations, are not always as they appear. Thankfully!

Judging by first appearances is, as they used to say, "for the birds".

Friday — October 6

BELIEVE it or not, some people smile with a straight face! For some, feeling like they have to smile is an imposition. Some smile naturally and often. Some work at it. Some never do it.

What we all have in common is that being on the receiving end of a good smile can make our day!

Someone smiled at me once, crossing a road. It brought tears to my eyes because it was so pure and sincere.

Happy World Smile Day, everyone!

Saturday — October 7

ANDREA never liked social media. She thought it brought out the worst in people and probably should be restricted.

Then she had a big operation scheduled. In the weeks before, she typed out her worries and fears. Friends from around the world sent her love and encouragement.

She got through it. She would have got through it anyway, but talking it out with other people made the process so much easier.

Social media sites are like every other invention ever – as bad or as good as the people who use them.

Sunday — October 8

I HEARD a parent ask his daughter what she was learning in school. "Health," she replied.

"Does it make you want to eat more vegetables?" he asked.

Her enthusiastic reply was, "Broccoli! Eww!"

Later, I saw a message from a church leader.

One follower was incensed, saying, "He just isn't a real believer!"

We shouldn't follow blindly, but neither should we dismiss the opinions of those who study such things.

Sometimes the biggest problem is overcoming our preconceptions about faith – or broccoli!

Are we open-minded enough to grow? Or will we keep insisting that vegetables aren't good for us?

Monday — October 9

I **SAT** behind two women at a public meeting. They weren't speaking at the meeting; they were just interested in the outcome.

I was more interested in their body language.

At one point, one woman put her hand on the back of the other one's shoulder and rubbed gentle circles into it. The one being comforted was a grandmother, already a source of wisdom and comfort for two generations. The one doing the comforting was her mother!

Do we ever grow past the age of needing a comforting hand? Are we ever too old to offer one? I don't think so!

Tuesday — October 10

WE met for breakfast. He was frustrated.

His bosses talked about respect and dignity for all, but he still had to clean up their mess.

He said he had to rush off, and left his breakfast remains for the café staff, or me, to clear away.

F.W. Farrar, an Archdeacon of Westminster in the 19th century, wrote "Great principles find their proper issue in the faithful performance of the little duties."

Wednesday — October 11

THE construction workers had used explosives to level a layer of rock before house-building could begin.

For the next step, two diggers used pneumatic spikes to "peck" at the bigger rock debris, breaking it down into rubble that would be used for landfill.

Because the diggers were working face to face, my ten-year-old companion said, "They look like two yellow dinosaurs having a fight!"

I happened to know that little fossils had been found in the area previously.

As much as we have moved on, perhaps the world isn't really all that different. In a child's eye, anyway!

Thursday — October 12

ONE woman was fairly successful in business, and the other described herself as a part-time volunteer for a well-known charity.

"Oh, so you're just a little cog in a big machine," the first woman said.

"Yes," the second woman replied, a little bemused. "But do you know what happens if you take a little cog out of a machine? It stops!"

Let's hear it for the little cogs who keep everything turning!

Friday — October 13

A CHILD I know showed his mother a video clip on his tablet. A little confused, his mother asked if it was real.

"It's better than real," the child insisted. "It's imaginary!"

She was about to tell him that that wasn't how the world worked. Then she thought about all the inventions that had to be imagined before they could ever be created.

Too often we think of imaginary things as being flighty and insubstantial.

Instead, she decided to let her son keep believing in the power of imagination – and wait to see where it leads!

Saturday — October 14

I CAME across a jar of smiles. It was a big surprise,
But being in an adventurous mood, I tried one on for size.
The smile felt great, I have to say; it cheered me up, I found,
And so I went out for a walk to share the smiles around.
I smiled at Naz, my neighbour, and the lad across the road,
The postie as she did her rounds, a gardener as he mowed.
I smiled at people in the park, at customers in the shop
And drivers at the traffic lights whose cars were at a stop.
Alas, my plan to give away the smiles was not to be,
As every time I smiled at folk, they just smiled back at me.

Ewan Smith

Little cogs are just as important as the bigger ones.

Sunday — October 15

IN 1863, Louisa May Alcott (author of "Little Women") published "Hospital Sketches", telling of her adventures as a Civil War nurse.

She focused mainly on the positives in these encounters, which upset some readers, who thought she ought to have treated the subject more sombrely.

To them, she responded: "It is a part of my religion to look well after the cheerfulness of life, and let the dismals shift for themselves, believing . . . that it is wise to be 'merrie in God'."

I do like that sort of wisdom!

Monday — October 16

THERE'S a joke where a mother is teaching her son table manners. He asks which school she learned motherhood at.

"There's no such thing as mummy school," she replies.

"Where did you learn all the rules?" he asks.

It's an under-appreciated fact that most parents make it up along the way, often without help, scrambling to get it right and hurting when they get it wrong.

If this helps you appreciate your parents more, I'm delighted.

If it helps you forgive them for the hurts they caused, then that's good, too.

Tuesday — October 17

JIM tucked the warm blanket around his granddaughter's shoulders and asked if she'd had a good day.

"Yes, Papa Jim. Why?" she replied.

"Because my favourite way to fall asleep is to think about the best things that happened that day. What was your favourite thing today?"

"Papa Jim . . ." She spoke hesitantly. "Gran's my favourite."

"Ouch!" I said when he told me this. "How did you respond?"

"The only way I could," he replied. "I told her that's as it should be. Then I kissed her head."

Wednesday — October 18

AT least once a year, George and Helen travel thousands of miles to visit their grandchildren.

"We do it so we'll be remembered," Helen said, laughing. "I hope that doesn't sound too vain."

It didn't sound vain at all. Why else do we live if not to have some sort of influence on the lives of others? Those influences are mostly of the guiding sort, the advising sort, the good example sort.

To be remembered for its own sake is pointless. To be a safe place, a guiding hand, and a reassuring word – that is precious!

Thursday — October 19

WE were standing in some manicured parkland, Morag told me of the railway lines that used to run there and the hump-backed bridges that crossed them.

"I remember pushing my great-gran in her wheelchair," she told me. "Those bridges were a challenge!"

Her great-gran's marriage certificate, she told me, was signed with a cross. Girls were uneducated back then, but she made sure her daughter went to school, and her granddaughter became a teacher.

"What was your job before you retired?" I asked.

"Inspector of Schools," she replied, smiling.

Education – isn't it wonderful? And women who want better than they had for their children – aren't they amazing?

Friday — October 20

ALICE CARY was a 19th-century American poet.

"It is not just as we take it, this mystical world of ours!" she wrote. "Life's field will yield, as we make it, a harvest of thorns or flowers!"

This world will offer many restrictions and disappointments when it comes to getting the life we want, but how we deal with them, by leaving them as thorns or turning them into flowers, will play a large part in shaping the life we end up with.

Go for flowers!

Saturday — October 21

I WAS walking in a new neighbourhood. I'd circled some unfamiliar streets, then I spotted the house I was staying in.

As I approached, I knew I hadn't done the number of paces I'd hoped for, but it was cold. I wanted to keep walking, but part of me was done. Each step brought me closer to temptation. I knew I would succumb.

Then I saw a path to the side. I took it, turned a corner, and, before my weaker nature could complain, I found myself back on the circuit, walking it again in the opposite direction!

The battle is real. Part of us will always want to give in to temptation.

Thank goodness for the providential side lanes and diversions that reinforce our better angels!

Sunday — October 22

CAROLANNE and Brian visited LOVE Park in Philadelphia.

There's a statue of the word "LOVE" there. They took a picture of themselves standing beneath it and posted it on social media.

In the next few minutes they had "likes" from the UK, the US, India, Australia, Hong Kong, Germany and the Philippines.

"It was a bigger, faster response than my posts usually get," Carolanne said. "It goes to show how keen the whole world is for a message of love."

As it goes: "A new commandment I give unto you, That ye love one another; as I have loved you, that ye also love one another."

Monday — October 23

HIS life's journey had been a downwards one. Seeking to find happier things to talk about, I asked where his home was.

"That's a difficult one," he replied.

Talking to the Lady Of The House afterwards, I said, "I wasn't expecting that for an answer."

"That," she told me, "is because you have lived a blessed life."

Home. I hope we all know where it is, was, or will be.

Tuesday — October 24

DO you know those people who always take a cynical view of life because, somehow, they know something the others don't?

Do you know those people who always take a sunshine-and-roses view of life because, somehow, they know something the others don't?

Each thinks they are right, and are prepared to base their life on that stance. There is no independent arbiter prepared to step in to say which is the correct view.

In the end, you make your own choice.

Given that, my question is: why would anyone choose anything other than happiness and love?

Wednesday — October 25

THE dog ran to meet the guest.

Thinking she wanted a treat, the guest held his hands out and said, "Sorry, girl. I don't have anything for you."

Then the dog's ten-year-old owner, with all the innocence of youth and not realising the profundity of her words, said, "You do. You have hands. You could comfort her with them."

May our hands never be so empty that they have no comfort for another creature in them.

Thursday — October 26

IF I asked you what was the kindest or most beautiful thing a celebrity had ever done for you, you might be stuck for an answer.

If I asked you what was the most wonderful thing an ordinary person had ever done for you, I'm sure you could tell me.

Playwright Alan Bennett, in his memoir "Writing Home", recalled seeing an orchestra going home after performing great classical pieces to an audience of thousands.

They were on the bus, exhausted, some heading to rented digs. It confirmed for him that the sublime could come from the ordinary.

Indeed, I've never looked anywhere else for real kindness, real beauty or real wonder!

Friday — October 27

HIS intentions are good. He drops his son off at school, seeing him off with a cheery wave.

He drives a small car and parks in the same place every weekday, but he always parks with his back wheel on the kerb.

It's a low, sloping kerb, so he might not notice, but the concrete has cracked just at that one spot. And, today, a little piece fell out. In the future, who knows?

His intentions are good. But this is how bad habits sneak up on us, little by little, making no difference, until one day, when finally the concrete cracks.

Saturday — October 28

WE were reminiscing about childhood treats.

Irene told me that every Saturday when she was little, her dad would bring home a Mars bar.

With great ceremony, he would cut it into six slices: one for him, one for Mum, one each for the two boys, and one for Irene.

"But that's only five," I protested.

"Ah," she said through a wide smile, "The sixth slice was stuck between the bars of the budgie's cage!"

I couldn't imagine many children these days being happy with a sixth of a Mars bar, but for Irene it would be a taste of childhood.

Sunday — October 29

SHE was visiting grandchildren in another country.

After the first day, Gran had the honour of tucking the little ones in for the night.

Having said his usual prayers, her grandson added: "And God bless Gran. Oh, God, did you know she's here on holiday?"

Her heart warmed, Gran paraphrased Psalm 139.

"'If I take wings in the morning'– which I did – 'and dwell in the uttermost part of the sea' – I flew across the ocean – 'even there shall thy hand lead me, and thy right hand shall hold me'. He knows, my darling."

Monday — October 30

HAVE you ever been to a pot-luck supper? Usually, it's a gathering of friends, relatives and neighbours.

Everyone brings some food, usually in casserole dishes or Tupperware containers.

It would have been in pots in days gone by, as that was all most kitchens had.

It is still pretty much pot luck what foodstuffs you end up with.

Another similarly named tradition exists.

"Potlatch" was a Native American feast, where the host's wider family would all contribute, and the success of the event would be dictated by the apparent generosity of the host.

The giving away of food or property to other members of the tribe might enhance status, get people on the host's side, or even be an apology for some transgression.

Different people did it for different reasons, but it was open for all to do. Community and order were maintained through generosity and hospitality.

It might have been abused from time to time, but in its purest form, I'd chance my luck – pot luck or otherwise – with that!

Tuesday — October 31

IT may be ancient philosophy, but it was a friend who first related it to me.

"Imagine being in a dark space," he said, "and a thin shaft of light appears. Then a moth flies into the beam and out the other side.

"You might be forgiven for thinking the moth had simply blinked into existence and disappeared again. It was only lit for a moment, but it actually had a before and an after."

The point of the original story escaped me, but I couldn't help but think of the judgements we pass on others based on the events of a fleeting moment.

That moment might have been difficult, but they (and we) have a before and an after.

Never close the door to the possibilities of a unfortunate cause, or a better tomorrow. They might regret the moment as well.

November

Wednesday — November 1

IN his book "Sir Gibbie", Scottish author George MacDonald suggested the secret to happiness might be found by examining our pets more closely.

"The bliss of the animals," he wrote, "lies in this . . . they shadow the bliss of those . . . who do not 'look before and after, and pine for what is not', but live in the holy carelessness of the eternal now."

I'm not saying to pay no heed to the future, or spend no time revisiting the past, where things might have been better. I suggest we spend more time in the here and now, where things are pretty fine.

Thursday — November 2

I LET myself into Joe's house. I found him sitting in his home office, a computer screen in front of him.

After our hellos, I started reminiscing about country churches in the days when they were candlelit and felt like ice-boxes in winter.

Folk would bring their dogs to the services, and the dogs would lie across their feet as the minister preached, keeping their toes toasty.

Joe wondered what I was talking about at first. Then he looked under his desk to where his German shepherd lay across his feet.

Many things have changed over the years, but some things have stayed the same.

Friday — November 3

OWAIN is not yet two. His speech has progressed from single words to phrases, and his latest is, "You need a hand?"

His parents thought it was cute. I thought it was more than that.

"Think of it this way," I explained. "Children copy what they hear. It seems that one of the phrases Owain hears most often is an offer of help. If only every child had that sort of start to life!"

144

Some things
never change.

Saturday — November 4

IN his 1860 book "The Conduct Of Life", writer Ralph Waldo Emerson mentioned "the Spirit of the Times".

Defining this spirit was a great topic of debate in Boston, New York and London. So what did Emerson think of it?

He wrote: "To me, however, the question of the times resolved itself into a practical question . . . How shall I live?"

There are many causes worth getting involved in, but we shouldn't let them distract us from this essential question.

How shall we live? What kind of people shall we be?

Sunday — November 5

JONATHAN often talks of his childhood, and his dad features strongly in those stories. They have a host of memories together.

Today, I sat next to him in church.

When the pastor said, "Let us pray," Jonathan called his very active son over.

The nine-year-old stood by his father's knees, they held hands, prayed, then off he ran.

Nothing much to it. But I do believe moments like those will be the times his son will tell his own children about in years to come.

Monday — November 6

JEANETTE fought a long battle with cancer. Throughout the process, she kept her cousin Ginny informed by e-mail.

Ginny's responses were always upbeat and supportive, but she must have worried.

It was with great relief that Jeanette was able to tell her she had the all-clear.

After replying to the good news, her cousin signed off with a phrase Jeanette had never heard before.

"Thank you," Ginny wrote, "for washing my face with happiness!"

Jeanette had to read it a few times before she understood.

Have you ever heard a more beautiful description of crying?

Tuesday — November 7

HE passed away 10 years ago. I have many memories of him, and I have one of his social media posts engraved on an ornamental slate.

It reads, "Here is love. Here is the presence of God."

He never explained it. Did he mean God is where love is?

Alternatively, did he mean that love and God are always "here", wherever we might be?

Not having the answer might be frustrating, but it does make me wonder every time I read it.

God and love stay at the forefront of my thoughts. Perhaps that was his plan all along.

Wednesday — November 8

ERNST HAAS was an Austrian-American photojournalist. His book, "The Creation", was one of the biggest selling photobooks ever.

He knew a thing or two about taking a good photo, and no-one could deny he had an eye for beauty.

"If the beautiful were not in us," he once said, "how would we ever recognise it?"

Think about that for a moment. Try to recall a beautiful thing you saw. Did it not tug at something within you?

Could it be that we, ourselves, are as beautiful as the most beautiful thing we ever saw?

Thursday — November 9

MY friend Allan is in the habit of leaving the house early most mornings to buy the newspapers and something for breakfast.

In summer, it's a positive delight. The sky will be rosy and the birds will be singing before many townsfolk have stirred from their beds. In winter, it can be a very different story.

"Beautiful days don't always come to you easily," he told me. "Sometimes you have to walk towards them."

Anything worth having is worth putting something of ourselves into. Meet the day halfway!

Friday — November 10

SOME sports are associated with rowdy, unpleasant crowds, and it's largely taken for granted. But it doesn't have to be that way.

A friend from Pennsylvania supports the Penn State American football team. He tells me that fans on one side of the stadium will often chant, "We are! We are! We are!"

Fans on the other side will reply, "Penn State! Penn State! Penn State!"

But it gets better!

At the end of the game, the fans on one side will shout, "Thank you!", and the fans on the other side will reply, "You're welcome!"

Who says you can't be loud and passionate, but still be polite?

Saturday — November 11

THERE'S a story told about science-fiction writer Robert A. Heinlein.

He was once approached by an appreciative fan who said Heinlein had given the world so much that he, the fan, would like to give something back.

Heinlein gently corrected him.

"You don't pay back," he said. "You pay forward."

He had a way with words, Mr Heinlein.

Take the love and appreciation you feel when you receive in a time of need and use it to help someone else.

Sunday — November 12

WE stood for the two minutes' silence in church. No-one moved or spoke – except for three-year-old Caleb.

He did a little shuffling dance, chatted to himself, and even, while his parents tried to shush him, broke into song.

I thought it was entirely appropriate. Why shouldn't a child's voice be heard at that time?

The best tribute we can pay to the fallen is to create a world where no more children are born to die on a battlefield somewhere.

Monday — November 13

DID you thank anyone today? We do it often, but what do we mean by it?

"Thank" comes from the same linguistic root as the word "think".

Originally, if someone performed a kindness for us, we assured them we would often think of them. They would have our "thinks", which gradually became "thanks".

Next time you offer someone your thanks, spend time thinking kindly of them as well.

Tuesday — November 14

I'VE been a "Doctor Who" fan from the beginning. In one episode, the Doctor confronts an alien about to unleash war on the world.

He asks her to stand down. She won't, because there would be consequences for her if she does not see her plan through.

The Doctor responds, "Look at me; I'm unforgivable. Well, here's the unforeseeable. I forgive you!"

He steps away from ego, away from retribution, and repeats, "I forgive you."

I'm not suggesting we battle aliens or stop wars, but perhaps we could be "the unforeseeable" in more local, more personal, conflict.

Forgiveness. It's what the doctor ordered.

Wednesday — November 15

I LOVE my little flat: it is, for me, the ideal home.
Although I live here by myself, I never feel alone.
I'm glad that, from my window, I can see the busy street
Where people park their cars or walk their dogs and tend to meet.
It's good to have a friendly chat and pass the time of day,
Take parcels in or water plants for those across the way.
I hear the children's laughter echo up and down the stair
And familiar footsteps overhead mean someone's always there.
Good neighbours help each other out – on that we can rely –
There's nowhere else I'd rather live, and they're the reason why.

Laura Tapper

Thursday — November 16

I HEARD the little girl say, "Grampa, you're silly!"
He responded, "Evie, I love you."

Evie moved closer and hugged his leg.

"I love you, too, Grampa," she said in a much softer tone. "And when I said 'silly', I meant it in a nice way!"

I don't think there is a nice way to tell someone they're silly. But I do think his unexpectedly loving response made her wish there was!

Try it. It works on children and adults.

Friday — November 17

WHEN Robert Louis Stevenson, author of "Treasure Island" and "Kidnapped", was hiking through France with his pack on a donkey, he came upon a religious institution in the mountains.

Because he had been raised in a differing, sometimes opposing, tradition, he approached it with more than a little concern.

He was tempted to walk on by, but there was no other shelter for the night.

After lodging there for a few days, he left, having been thoroughly charmed by every one of its residents.

We don't help anyone – least of all ourselves – when we see people as "labels". People are people, in every tradition.

Saturday — November 18

WHEN I think of Friedrich Nietzsche, the German philosopher who helped shape the thinking of the western world, I think of big books and an equally big moustache.

The man's wisdom was beyond my understanding in so many fields.

Apparently, he also said, "Without music, life would be a mistake", and observed that you can't both be a pessimist and play the flute.

Knowing he had a love of music and a sense of humour is almost enough to encourage me to tackle one of his books. Almost!

THERE is an old German parable of two travellers arriving at a village. As they sit by the well to rest, the inn catches fire.

The first traveller says, "That's awful, but nothing to do with us."

The second traveller rushes to help salvage goods and save people.

Afterwards, the first traveller asks, "Who bade you risk your life like that?"

The second traveller responds, "He who bids me bury a seed, that it may grow and multiply and bring forth increase."

The first traveller dryly observes, "Well, if that inn had collapsed, it would have buried you."

"Then I would have become the seed," the second traveller replies.

A SECRET of kindness? For me, it's understanding that I don't know enough.

People who tend towards rudeness or unkindness usually think they know enough, to justify releasing some "deserved" unpleasantness into the situation.

I usually find I don't know enough about the person, or the situation, to do that.

Sometimes taking the time to learn a little more encourages the other person to be more giving. I don't know much, but I do know that sometimes not knowing enough can be enough.

THE earliest known autobiography written in English is "The Book Of Margery Kempe". It tells us much about the life of an ordinary person in 15th-century England.

It also raises a lot of questions for the modern reader. However, the introduction warns that it may disappoint the reader unless, "he is careful to ask from it only those things which it can give him".

I read those words and thought them wonderful advice, too, for when we deal with one another.

ON a visit to New York, I splurged six dollars on a NYC baseball cap. I handed over what I thought were six dollar bills and took my cap.

A hundred yards down the street, he caught up with me, having abandoned his stall. I'd given him five dollar bills – and one hundred dollar bill!

Back then, New York was seen as a place where everyone was out for themselves. Real life proved that wrong.

Never judge – a city, or a group of people. Honest folk are everywhere!

Thursday — November 23

NICOLE wasn't happy with her son's school, so she went to meetings and tried to get things changed – to no avail.

Frustrated, she complained to her husband – a pastor – about his lack of support.

Frank heard the upset in her voice and said, "Let's take some of that passion and redirect it towards setting up a church school."

We all have the option to redirect our passions. If one way isn't working, don't go down the road of anger and bitterness – find a better way. If your idea is deserving of your passion, you can be sure there will be a better way!

Friday — November 24

THE tree in my neighbour's garden is not a local species. It has been preparing for winter like the others. Its leaves are similar to a maple's and turn a bronze colour. When these leaves fall, they don't do it randomly, but in strict order, from the top down.

Right now, four-fifths of the 30-feet-high tree are bare. The branches at the bottom still have their whole complement of leaves.

It puzzled me for a moment, then I saw the sense. Nutrition rises. The lower branches are the first – and last – stop for all good stuff.

I guess that's what we mean when we advise people to stay close to their roots!

Cities can be full of surprises.

153

Saturday — November 25

A **BUSY** *day has ended*
With hours full of fun;
Eyes are very sleepy now,
As nightfall has begun.
Our cosy beds are waiting
To dream the night away.
Thank you, God, for all your care,
Throughout this precious day.

Avril Hooper

Sunday — November 26

THE arch of cut stone where wall met pavement helped explain the rectangle of ground-level concrete in front of it.

This had once been an entrance to a basement.

After the concrete set, someone had taken something rough to the surface and, in large cursive letters, scratched the word "Love".

There are other ways of telling that the building is a church, but that one word – impromptu but appropriate – is my favourite!

Monday — November 27

MOVIE star Arnold Schwarzenegger tells a story of being hospitalised with measles as a child. His roommate had a banana.

Young Arnold had never tasted a banana.

He asked for the peel, and scraped tiny bits of fruit off the inside, and to this day it remains one of the most delicious things he has ever tasted.

How many things in life do we take for granted because of our familiarity with them?

If only we could recall the first time for each of them, and re-experience those early sensations in the same way!

Imagine, if you will, those first, intense experiences making you the classic Arnie promise.

"I'll be back!"

Tuesday — November 28

I HEARD of an architect who designed magnificent Gothic buildings. There seemed to be no rhyme nor reason to the placement of the windows. He only placed them where he thought sunlight would be needed, or where they might look out to a view he liked.

He might see beautiful sunsets from a window, but only at the right time of year. He might not have wanted to look at bare fields, and so miss them being full of waving corn.

We do ourselves a disservice when we limit what we look at. Look for life to change, and look to find the beauty in every direction.

Wednesday — November 29

I THANKED my hostess for the bar of soap she left out for me.

"You're welcome," she replied. "But it's an odd thing to single out."

"Ah, well, yes," I agreed. "But I'm sure I put you out in lots of ways, and you did a hundred little things for me that I was completely unaware of. Saying thanks for the soap was my way of saying thanks for all the other things as well."

In the course of an ordinary day, lots of people will perform little courtesies for us that we might miss. Appreciating the kindnesses we are unaware of seems like common sense.

Thursday — November 30

WILLIAM lives from month to month money-wise. He usually has a little cash to spare, but it wouldn't take much to wipe it out.

Recently, a couple of minor catastrophes used up his savings.

Into this situation I stepped, asking for donations for charity. He took out his wallet and made a substantial donation.

Once I knew of his situation, I tried to give the money back.

"Please don't," he replied. "If you do, I'll try to eke it out and worry all the while. Now I have nothing, I have nothing to worry about. I'll be happier living in trust that everything will work out."

I thought his attitude beautiful, and set about doing what I could to make sure everything would work out for a kind-hearted man.

Make a wish!

December

IN 1778, Henry Walton painted a scene of an old sailor selling ballads on the street. In it, the ballads he wrote were pinned to a board and a young woman was looking through them.

In pre-television and radio days, entertainment occurred in the parlour and was largely self-made. Perhaps the young woman would sing the ballad to friends and family. Perhaps another family member would accompany her on the pianoforte.

And all because an old sea-dog wrote a song down.

We need not be beautiful to add beauty to the world. We need not be a singer to play music. We need not be able to write a song to sing it well.

If we each do what we can, and let others put their talents into the mix, the resulting beauty will be more than any one of us could manage on our own.

Saturday — December 2

FOR some reason, a late dandelion sprouted in my neighbours' garden and went full-on puff-ball.

By the time their children saw it, the dew had bedecked it, then the cold had frozen the dew.

They gathered cardboard from their parents' recycling bin – Sarah, six; Max, four; and the twins, Angel and Nial, eight – and lay on top of it, in a circle on the grass around the glistening weed.

At first I thought they were admiring its beauty. Then I realised they were breathing on it.

Sarah saw me looking over the fence and waved.

"We're being the sun," she explained. "Once we've melted the frost, we'll be the wind."

I watched, entranced, as the fine frost melted and the revived seeds took flight on a breeze made of the breath of little children.

Sunday — December 3

I AM 'T-Shirt Michael'," the brother of a friend said by way of introduction. "I paint T-shirts. Sometimes I paint T-shirts for children, but I'm always painting them for God."

It would be easy to dismiss such a statement as wacky, but I liked it for two reasons.

Firstly, Michael knows who he is and what he is all about. His T-shirt artwork is beautiful – it is worth being known by.

Secondly, religious men and women throughout the centuries have performed works of all sorts – some great and others lowly – in the name of God.

I don't think God cares what we do, so long as we do our best, do it from love, and understand that, whatever it is, we do it because God enabled us.

I have two questions. Who are we in God? And what are we doing for God?

Monday — December 4

DESPITE being almost ninety years old, the book was in fine condition. It was full of stories of encouragement and wise words from times gone by. They seemed quite quaint by today's standards.

There was nothing in the main text of the book to indicate anyone had taken particular note. No dog-eared pages or underlines.

However, a small paragraph in the introduction was bracketed by pencilled asterisks.

It read: "Friend, I cannot take the burden from your shoulders – would to God that I could. I cannot make the road less rough or the hill less steep.

"But, see, there is a long way to travel still. I will go with you if you will have me, and together we will talk of whatsoever things are lovely that perhaps a little good cheer may drop into our hearts."

The stories and *bon mots* that comprise the book never seem to have achieved what the author did by reaching out, by understanding that life is difficult and best not walked alone.

Circumstances may make us solitary, but our hearts reach always outwards.

Offer a hand. Let yours be held. Walk together.

Tuesday — December 5

BRIAN has a baseball cap with an embroidered heart on the front. Not a love heart – an actual heart! I had to find out why.

He'd been at the Franklin Institute museum in Philadelphia.

They have many interactive visitor exhibits there, including an illuminated "brain" (actually a rope climbing frame) for children to climb through, and a similar set-up with a heart.

"They call it the Giant Heart," Brian told me. "That's what's on the cap. I can't think of a better way to meet people than by presenting them with a great big heart."

Wednesday — December 6

IN a letter written in 1818, poet John Keats talks of the intricate wonder of a spider's web.

He notes that this masterpiece of design – on the inside – is supported by very few anchor points.

The next time I saw a web, picked out in the morning frost, I looked for what he described.

Sure enough, the web was anchored to the garden fence, the handle of a shovel, a branch and a bin. Four points of security, but within that, an "airy citadel".

We might not have many things we can depend on in life, but the measure of us will be what we can build between them.

Thursday — December 7

TIME is inexorable. It passes and there is nothing we can do about it. Or so it seems.

Richard Jefferies, the 19th-century nature writer, suggested a means of temporary escape when he said: "The hours when the mind is absorbed by beauty are the only hours when we really live, so that the longer we can stay among these things so much the more is snatched from inevitable Time."

It's perhaps not strictly true, but having spent those hours with beauty, would we feel like complaining? Or might we feel that time had stood still a while?

The enthusiastic innocence of dogs never fails to bring a smile.

Friday — December 8

*R*EMEMBER *the wonder of Christmas*
When we were very young?
The air was filled with magic,
As Christmas songs were sung.

Excitement entered everywhere,
And made each day worthwhile.
The lights and decorations
Each gave us all a smile.

Perhaps we can recapture
That special time we knew,
And let the magic lift our hearts,
Still there for me and you.

Iris Hesselden

Saturday — December 9

I **AM** not unfailingly cheerful! There are many days when I get out of bed with a creak and a groan.

Do you know what sets me up for the day? A golden retriever.

My neighbour is a teacher, and out of the house for most of the day, so while she's at work, I dog-sit.

Each working day I unlock the kitchen door to let my doggy friend out.

No matter what mood I might be in before the door opens, she will always greet me with a stretch and a yawn.

After that, she'll bound across and sit to attention, head up, waiting eagerly to be told she is a good girl.

Now, I could still be grumpy, but such enthusiastic innocence asks more of me – asks better of me.

We might think there's not much of that sort of enthusiasm to be found in the world these days.

Instead, I think, just as she encourages me, so, too, we might encourage each other.

Let's take some of that enthusiastic innocence for "walkies", and watch it run.

Sunday — December 10

"THE Peasant Poet", written by John Clare, tells of the mundane things in the life of a countryman: the streams, the clouds, the birds, the storms – even the insects in the pond.

It tells of his appreciation of all of those things as creations of God.

His life was ordinary, but he understood that ordinariness as something more.

"A silent man in life's affairs, a thinker from a boy, a peasant in his daily cares, a poet in his joy."

Living like that would, I believe, be a very acceptable form of worship.

Monday — December 11

WHEN we think of the mind having powers, we might think of telepathy or telekinesis.

Essayist Charles Montague had something no less wonderful in mind when he wrote of a mind power that children and artists have:

"The power of taking delight in a thing, or rather in anything, everything, not as a means to some other end, but just because it is what it is."

We were all children once. Do you remember that power?

Montague's good news was that it need not be lost, not to the end of their days, by anyone who has ever had it.

It's still there. Dig it out and appreciate it for what it is.

Tuesday — December 12

THE English poet Leigh Hunt left us these words on contentment.

"Few people, rich or poor, make the most of what they possess. In their anxiety to increase the amount of the means for future enjoyment they are too apt to lose sight of the capability of them for present. Above all, they overlook the thousand helps to enjoyment which lie about them, free to everybody, and obtainable by the very willingness to be pleased."

He wasn't saying don't plan for the future. He was suggesting we make more of the here and now.

Wednesday — December 13

THE back hall of the church had cardboard boxes lined up in rows outside its door.

Volunteers went in and out, filling the boxes with recommended foods for a single person, couple or family. Each box held enough to last for three days.

They were lined up outside because the hall itself was full of food donated by people who didn't want anyone to go hungry. Once the essentials were boxed, a donated treat went in along with them.

The spirit of Christmas was very much in evidence in those unadorned parcels.

Thursday — December 14

IN his book "Dream Children", English essayist Charles Lamb wrote about visiting his grandmother's house.

Its hallway held marble busts of the Twelve Caesars who ruled Rome. The gardens were vast, populated by fruit trees and the occasional gardener.

My gran's hallway had a pantry at the end in which she kept food and coal. Her garden was a drying green with a path made of ashes left from the coal fire.

Yet I think we would both have looked back on those childhood visits with the same warm feeling.

There was one common ingredient that added the magic to our memories: grandmothers!

Friday — December 15

WE often hear of snowflakes being beautifully and uniquely designed, as if they were somehow exceptional.

When Henry David Thoreau, writer and student of the natural world, commented on this, he said, "Nature is full of genius, full of the divinity; so that not a snowflake escapes its fashioning hand."

Not even a snowflake. Amazing as they might be, snowflakes could easily be amongst the least spectacular of nature's miracles.

Isn't that a thought to inspire?

Saturday — December 16

TODAY is the Day of Reconciliation in South Africa. It marks the ending of apartheid in a spirit of reconciliation rather than a spirit of retribution.

Reconciling differences instead of perpetuating them has to be the best way to go in almost every situation. I'm sure we all agree, in theory.

In practice, it is no easy walk. Reconciling with someone we have fallen out with is often more than many can manage.

It's a high ideal. We're always at our best when reaching for those.

Sunday — December 17

FOUR-YEAR-OLD Evie asked her dad one of those questions that parents dread: "Are Jesus and Santa friends?"

Imagine being put on the spot like that! How would you answer?

Her dad could see why she might think they were. Both are kind and both want children to be good. Both give gifts – Jesus in a more universal sense; Santa in a date-specific sense.

He tells me he side-stepped the complexities of the question and went for the most straightforward answer he could think of.

"Jesus is everyone's friend!"

Monday — December 18

AN empty house had baked beans thrown at its window. I passed it a month or so later when a young man was hard at work.

He confessed he might have had something to do with it.

"It was a laugh at first," he said. "We thought someone would have to clean them off, but the they just hung there, streaking the window. Eventually they turned black and got harder. I thought they might put someone who needed a house off living there.

"So . . ." He held up the windscreen scraper and baby wipes he was using by way of explanation.

Acting on the impulse of an excited moment is one thing, but time to think about our actions often casts a different light on them.

I think a lesson might have "bean" learned for the future.

Christmas is a time for kindness and friendship.

Tuesday — December 19

SOMEONE talked to me recently of the patience it took to put up with "angular individuals".

"You know," he explained, "people who are all awkward corners and are never pleased with anything. They're a real trial to me."

What if he wasn't patient, this friend of mine? Would he, even temporarily, become as angular as them?

You see, they are often as they are because of disappointment, or have been hurt early in life. They truly believe their behaviour to be the only proper response to an unkind world.

What they think they want is for others to behave similarly and justify their approach.

We can take refuge in patience and in generosity, no matter how much they try us.

They may leave, and it will seem that all our efforts will have been for nothing. But they will have seen the world be kind.

At some level, they will know there is another way!

Wednesday — December 20

THOSE of us who are less nautical might never have heard the term "sheet anchor".

The dictionary defines it as a large, strong anchor, carried on a ship in case of emergency. Someone who can be relied on in troubled times.

The term has even entered into the financial world. There are sheet anchor investments that are supposedly more reliable than most.

During the Napoleonic Wars, the Royal Marines were referred to as the sheet anchor of Great Britain.

The sheet anchor would be carried near the middle of the ship, and for almost every voyage it would simply be there. If the regular anchors, usually to the fore or to the aft, failed, then everything would depend on the sheet anchor.

Being that kind of person in someone else's troubled life is a daunting prospect, but an honour.

Having someone like that in your own life – even if you never need to call on them – is a comfort beyond words.

Thursday — December 21

ON winter days, for centuries, people have gathered around fires and told stories, said prayers or sought magic.

For my young friend and me, wrapped in blankets after an early rise and sitting in front of a "fire" that was actually a TV screen, the fire-related topic of discussion was how to get in touch with Santa.

My little friend had an app on her tablet. She called it up and amended her wish-list. She also told Santa of the latest ways in which she might qualify for his Nice List and sent it off into the internet.

I told her of a little boy, kneeling in front of a coal fire, holding a handwritten note in a pair of tongs. Closer and closer to a real flame the paper would go, until he could feel the heat on his knuckles and the paper began to char and curl.

He would watch, entranced and hopeful, as paper and pencil markings turned into smoke and spiralled up the chimney.

Somehow, he knew, this smoke and the smoke from millions of other homes would make its way through the frosty air to the North Pole – where Santa would be able to read every word.

We sat there, together in a moment of silent wonder, as I wondered whose childhood really was the most magical.

Friday — December 22

WHEN I was a schoolboy, our whole class pulled a prank, then denied all knowledge of it.

Our headmaster – Mr Christian – lined us up and challenged us to be honest.

Then, that having failed, he stopped in front of me.

A little man, he looked up at me and softly said he knew me to be an honest boy, and if I said it was so then he would believe us all.

With my classmates listening nervously for my answer, I said our lie was the truth.

We were dismissed. We got away with it.

As an old man now, I still remember his face and his belief that I was honest. I didn't really get away with it.

An untruth might seem like a short-term advantage, but it can take a long-term toll.

Saturday — December 23

BUILDING a toy garage for a little boy, my mind drifted to Christmases of my childhood. It was a pleasant meander down Memory Lane.

But it felt like more – like being part of an old tradition. Older, even, than Christmas.

When I sought to put it into words, it felt like winter – not dormant, not still, but busily preparing the way for spring, as it always has done. As it always will.

Sunday — December 24

THE "Charlie Brown Christmas" special first aired in 1965. It has become an American television classic, but isn't so well known in the UK.

In it, Charlie Brown is disillusioned by the commercialisation of Christmas – yes, even back then!

He adopts a scrawny little Christmas tree and tries to prove it is as good as any other, but all he gets is ridiculed for his efforts.

Near despair, he asks, "Isn't there anyone who knows what Christmas is all about?"

His friend Linus offers to explain.

"And there were in the same country shepherds abiding in the field, keeping watch over their flock by night.

"And, lo, the angel of the Lord came upon them, and the glory of the Lord shone round about them, and they were sore afraid.

"And the angel said unto them: 'Fear not: for, behold, I bring you tidings of great joy, which shall be to all people.

"'For unto you is born this day in the city of David, a saviour, which is Christ the Lord.

"'And this shall be a sign unto you. Ye shall find the babe wrapped in swaddling clothes, lying in a manger'.

"And suddenly there was with the angel a multitude of the heavenly host praising God, and saying, 'Glory to God in the highest, and on Earth, peace, goodwill toward men'."

We might add our own variations, but the essential message is always the same.

Monday — December 25

ONE Christmas in the 1860s, American poet Henry Wadsworth Longfellow, recently become a widower, was nursing a son who had been shot during the American Civil War.

In response, he wrote the poem "Christmas Bells", more popularly known as the carol "I Heard The Bells On Christmas Day", with its insistent refrain of "Peace on earth, good will to men".

Should you be in your own personal winter, may the true spirit of Christmas reach out to you and lift you up.

Peace and goodwill – the bells still ring.

Tuesday — December 26

ON a day with nothing much else to do, let me ask, "How often do we try not to think?"

One friend listens to music through earphones wherever they go. Another prefers podcasts.

We might have the television on all day, or fill an empty house with voices from the radio. Some of us talk.

Do we think we might avoid thinking by doing these other things?

Of course, there are some things we would rather avoid thinking about, but they are still in there, occupying space and emotional effort, waiting to be noticed.

When I am out in the countryside with my doggy friend, and she knows where she's going, and there's nothing much to occupy my mind except looking around, these thoughts have a harder time being ignored.

Problems are faced, solutions are found (or, at least, steps are made towards finding them), and there is space for new thought to occur.

The feeling of good health after a long walk isn't just physical – it's mental and emotional as well.

Of course, going for long walks isn't an option everyone has, but, for the sake of mental health, let's find some way in the New Year of spending some safe, secure and relaxed time with our own thoughts.

Just thinking.

Wednesday — December 27

SCOTTISH poet Robert Fergusson referred to the period between Christmas Day and New Year's Day as "daft days". At a time when the world was dark, cold and dismal, he thought the only sensible response was to play music, dance, sing and indulge a little.

We are often at our best when times are difficult, and when the world would have us hibernate, celebrating seems both daft and sensible.

May we all rise to the challenge and enjoy the daft days – sensibly, of course!

Thursday — December 28

JOHN HADFIELD was an anthologist and a publisher.

As a young man he caught tuberculosis, which kept him in bed for many months. Thoughts of mortality, and what sort of husband and provider he might be if he lived, weighed heavily on his mind.

Enough to depress anyone, surely!

Instead, he found his mind dwelling more "in the joys of life, in the inexhaustible variety of the pleasures which my senses and sensibilities could still enjoy."

Later, he compiled a volume of pictures and prose that stirred his soul and called it simply "A Book Of Beauty".

Those of us who aren't in imminent danger of losing those wonders – how can we appreciate them any less?

Friday — December 29

STERLING. The word implies purity and integrity, but what does it mean?

It's thought to be a 13th-century word from when Britain traded extensively with the Baltic countries. Merchants from the east, these "Easterlings", used a silver coin of high purity and had a reputation for honesty.

Soon more and more people wanted paid in the Easterling way. The "ea" was dropped and "pounds sterling" entered our language.

Be more sterling. Pure, trusted and shining bright.

I'VE found a good size canvas
And I'm feeling quite inspired.
I've all the paints and brushes,
All the magic that's required:
A landscape, flowers, a street scene,
Abstract, seascapes and more.
The time's right for my favourite –
A glacial treat in store.
View's chosen and I'm ready
To catch the morning light.
The essence of stark silence
On the wonderland of white.
And, right on cue, there bobbing,
Sweet robin, breast aflame,
At home in the shining snowflakes,
Pirouetting down again.
Crisp meringue of freezing snow
And diamond wink of sun,
The pine trees, holly, berries,
My winter painting's done.

Dorothy McGregor

ONE of the joys of reading old books and letters is the discovery of words once in common usage but now no longer heard.

In Great-aunt Louisa's diary, she described the complicated work of a group of friends in a charitable cause as "weaving a tapestry empyrean".

Of course, I had to look it up.

"Empyrean", as Great-aunt Louisa seems to have used it, means the place where heaven and earth meet, the place where God's plan and people's plans are indistinguishable.

I would like to say it's a word I will use more often in everyday speech, but I would love to say it's a "place" I will visit more often in the year ahead.

Have a happy and blessed New Year.

Have an "empyrean" New Year!

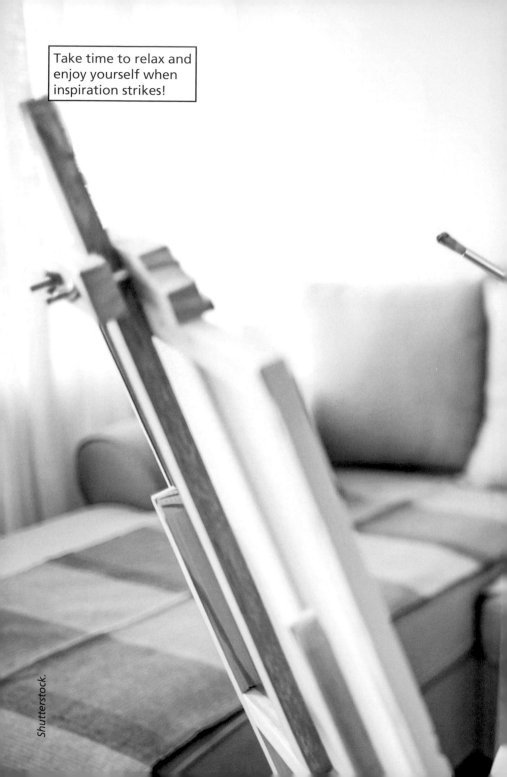

Take time to relax and enjoy yourself when inspiration strikes!

Shutterstock.

*"True friends are always
together in spirit"*

L.M. Montgomery